Andy & Me and the Hospital is a great read full of insights into how and why healthcare leaders must change. This book stays focused on the most important activities and behaviors leaders need to learn to create a culture of continuous improvement. Another home run by Pascal Dennis.

Dr. John Toussaint
Chief Executive Officer, ThedaCare Center for Healthcare Value

Pascal takes simple concepts and shows them in action in a manner that is both inspiring and challenging simultaneously. I plan to share copies of this book to help our organization achieve greater performance.

Dean Gruner, MD, MMM
President and CEO, ThedaCare

Pascal has described the path to superior and systemic management practices that are the way to unlock the transformational energy of the incredible people working in healthcare, and to achieve the level of operational excellence and the quality of care our patients deserve.

James Hereford
Chief Operating Officer, Stanford Health Care

An excellent overview of what it takes to truly embrace the Lean journey. A great read for those considering adopting Lean in their organization.

Norman Gruber
President and CEO, Salem Health (retired)

Dennis has written a great story of how Lean thinking can apply to one of the most complex systems in all of human activity, the acute care hospital. It is an engaging story, well-told with human faces and realistic problems. The questions at the end of each chapter encourage the reader to commit himself/herself to a position on the opinions expressed. Have I seen this behavior? Do I agree with that observation?

I learned a lot reading this book, and enjoyed it all the way. It shows how complex problems of large health systems can be tackled by an understandable systematic approach. Realistic problems they face include the lack of clarity of responsibility, the proliferation of top-down initiatives, and the silo mentality plaguing our healthcare institutions. Chapter 8 provides the best brief description I've seen of how strategy deployment (*hoshin kanri*) applies in healthcare.

Dr. John (Jack) Billi
Professor of Internal Medicine and Learning Health Sciences, Medical School; Associate Vice President for Medical Affairs, The University of Michigan Health System

Great story, easy read. Pascal Dennis presents the tools and, more importantly, the thinking necessary to apply the principles of TPS to the transformation of healthcare. A must read and permanent companion for the journey to improve healthcare.

John Fitzgerald
Chief Executive Officer, Inova Fair Oaks Hospital

Pascal gets to the heart of the process improvement challenge in healthcare, and paints a compelling picture of the cultural transformation journey. Pascal clearly describes the critical elements an organization must embrace, and the barriers that must be overcome to truly achieve healthcare excellence. Study questions at the end of each chapter enable rich reflection on where your organization is and where it can be.

Joe Pilon
Chief Operating Officer, Health Sciences North

A gift to all healthcare administrative and physician leaders, and a must read for ALL current and future leaders in training. This book translates the principles and concepts of TPS in a way that leaders at all levels can use. This book is their day-to-day companion on the journey to transform healthcare and get results that matter for our patients and staff.

Debbie Barnard
Vice President, Process Improvement, Quality and Patient Safety at Health Sciences North

Once again, Tom and Andy enter my life and change it for the better. And this time, our Lean adventurers find themselves in the least standardized, most variable, most complex organization on the planet: the modern hospital. Pascal Dennis is a master storyteller. He understands the deep human need for stories in order to see ourselves in real life situations and really learn. Tom and Andy show step-by-step how Lean, as a complete system of management and not just a bunch of tools, can transform any healthcare organization for better outcomes, lower costs and dramatically improved morale and engagement.

Dr. David Holloway
Chief Executive Officer, Bend Memorial Clinic

Andy & Me and the Hospital

Further Adventures on the Lean Journey

Pascal Dennis

CRC Press is an imprint of the
Taylor & Francis Group, an **informa** business
A PRODUCTIVITY PRESS BOOK

CRC Press
Taylor & Francis Group
6000 Broken Sound Parkway NW, Suite 300
Boca Raton, FL 33487-2742

Printed on acid-free paper
Version Date: 20160504

International Standard Book Number-13: 978-1-4987-4033-3 (Paperback)

Library of Congress Cataloging-in-Publication Data

Names: Dennis, Pascal, 1957- author.
Title: Andy & me and the hospital : further adventures on the lean journey / Pascal Dennis.
Other titles: Andy and me and the hospital
Description: 1 Edition. | Boca Raton : CRC Press, 2016. | Includes index.
Identifiers: LCCN 2015048106 | ISBN 9781498740333
Subjects: LCSH: Manufacturing processes--Fiction. | Medical care--Fiction. | Production management--Fiction. | Just-in-time systems--Fiction. | Production control--Fiction.
Classification: LCC PS3604.E5865 A536 2016 | DDC 813/.6--dc23
LC record available at https://lccn.loc.gov/2015048106

Visit the Taylor & Francis Web site at
http://www.taylorandfrancis.com

and the CRC Press Web site at
http://www.crcpress.com

Printed and bound in the United States of America by Publishers Graphics, LLC on sustainably sourced paper.

For my dear wife, Pamela, and for her dad,

the late great Dr. Robert Guselle.

We still miss you, Bob.

Contents

Preface

Why a book about Toyota methods (aka "Lean") in a *hospital*?

Because healthcare is a dark realm full of opportunity. If we don't get it right, it could bankrupt us.

Why *this* book?

I want to answer some basic questions. What does a Lean transformation in a hospital feel like? What overall approach should we take? What kind of leadership and behavior change is needed? How do we develop and engage people? How do we improve processes? How do we build a management system? How do we translate what Deming called the "profound system of knowledge"?

At the same time, I want to provide a clear and simple guide to Toyota methods and thinking, how they fit together, and the spirit that animates them. One of the problems with Lean implementation has been the tendency to cherry-pick activities, rather than grasping the system as a whole.

Why a sequel to *Andy & Me* and *The Remedy*?

People seem to like Tom Papas and Andy Saito. Their journey is perhaps a useful metaphor for leaders.

Change is hard; change hurts. At best we partially succeed, and that makes all the difference.

DISCLAIMER

The characters, situations, and organizations described herein are entirely fictional. Any similarity between these and actual people, situations, and organizations is purely coincidental.

Acknowledgments

I'm grateful to all the good people who have helped to make this book a reality, and I acknowledge them here.

Michael Sinocchi, executive editor; Jessica Vakili; and the Taylor & Francis team for their support all these years.

The Lean Pathways team with whom it is my privilege to work.

All my senseis over the years. (You know who you are.) I hope you will overlook this book's many shortcomings.

Dianne Caton, artist extraordinaire, with whom it's such a pleasure to collaborate.

Allen Sutterfield, my writing sensei, for his insight and light touch.

All our reviewers for their time and care.

Special thanks to Dr. Jack Billi for his invaluable insights and guidance.

The growing number of hospitals around the world that are in the midst of heartfelt process and cultural transformations. I'm lucky enough to work with some of you. You're fighting the good fight, and though it'll take a long time, you're going to win.

My dear wife, Pamela, and our children, Eleanor, Katie, and Matthew.

1

Why Do I Feel So Lousy?

"Maybe you've become addicted to stress," Sarah says.

I take a sip of bourbon. End of day. We're sitting in McSorley's looking out over the New York City skyline.

"You're a warrior," she said. "You're ready to die for what you believe in. I love that about you. But it's a hard way to live."

I'm forty-four years old and a big shot at last. Taylor Motors, Director of Manufacturing Operations—a *Domo*. My domain comprises four factories in the Northeast, including my alma mater, New Jersey Motor Manufacturing (NJMM), which people said I'd brought back from the dead. My personal life is better too. I've made peace with my ex-wife and remarried. Sarah teaches kindergarten in Hoboken, New Jersey, where we live in a fine brownstone overlooking Sinatra Drive and Pier A Park.

The Manhattan ferry is docking. Passenger ramps come down and people stream off. "I don't know, Sarah. I just feel lousy."

The Greeks have a word—*kefi*—that means zest, brio, the soul and body brimming over. *Kefi* is Zorba dancing on the beach in the film *Zorba the Greek*, or my cousins smashing plates at weddings. But I just feel stale, with no *kefi* at all.

Tom Papas is the name—*Papachristodoulou*. A Greek boy who made good, the restaurant rat who became a Domo. My mentor, Andy Saito, taught me to draw things out. Here's how I see the past decade (Figure 1.1).

Have I become addicted to turmoil? Am I incapable of enjoying a normal life? Sarah wants children, but I've been lukewarm to the idea. What am I afraid of? Another divorce? Or do I fear domesticity itself, the "normal" life? Am I happy only when unhappy (Figure 1.2)?

* *

I'm walking to my car in the NJMM parking lot. It's late September, my favorite time of year. The afternoon shift is off to a good start. I'm wearing my navy blue NJMM windbreaker celebrating our recent Gold Medal for Quality (Best Mid-size Sporty Car).

We've just completed our monthly status meeting. Rachel Armstrong, EVP North America, made me Northeast region Domo as a reward for our achievements. I oversee four factories in all—in New Jersey, Connecticut, Pennsylvania, and Ohio. Each month we meet at a different site and review our current condition across four focus areas—People, Quality, Delivery, and Cost.

I owe Rachel, big time. She's made it easy for me to stay close to my girls, Sophie and Helen, who live with their mother on Manhattan's Upper East Side. Rachel has saved me from firing at least twice.

Each factory is making its numbers, making problems visible and working on root causes. There's less of the old Taylor song and dance. "Everything is just great. Everything is just great. Oh, by the way, we just fell off a cliff."

When I took over as Domo three years ago, I had to prune a great deal of deadwood. Not the front line team members, who are pretty solid, but managers, many of whom had the old Taylor Motors sense of entitlement: "I work at Taylor Motors

FIGURE 1.1

Tom and Andy's previous adventures. (*From Andy & Me—Crisis and Transformation on the Lean Journey*, 2nd ed. New York: Productivity Press, 2011, and *The Remedy—Bringing Lean Out of the Factory to Transform the Entire Organization*. New York: John Wiley & Sons, 2010.) Copyright 2015 Lean Pathways Inc.

FIGURE 1.2
Tom's discontent. Copyright 2015 Lean Pathways Inc.

and the world owes me a living." I found that incredible, given our experience over the past decade.

But has Taylor Motors culture really changed? As our profitability grows, I sense the old corporate antibodies awakening. I know Rachel is concerned about it. And I know that the Northeast region and I have our share of detractors, people who don't believe in the Toyota approach, despite our results.

Company cultures are strange that way. You get used to a certain way of thinking, a certain way of looking at the world, and it makes you oblivious to glaring problems. It's like we're wearing a set of glasses that filter and often distort reality.

How well do *I* see reality, I wonder?

My sensei has helped me see a little better. Takinori (Andy) Saito is a retired former Toyota heavyweight who lives in New Jersey. When we met, my life was a train wreck. Our factory was about to close down, and I was in the midst of my divorce.

"Some problems have no countermeasure, Tom-san," Andy said. "One day they just go away."

I didn't know that Andy had resigned from Toyota in despair and guilt over the loss of his wife, Shizuko. "She was my wife, my best friend, my biggest supporter," Andy told me. "But when she needed me I was not there."

My sensei paid a terrible price for his inattention. Would I make the same mistake? I knew I was prone to it.

Andy mentored me through the NJMM rescue, playing Virgil to my Dante. We've kept him on retainer for years now, and it's our best investment ever. I look forward to our monthly *gemba** walks followed by dinner and bourbon at the Iron Horse Tavern.

There's my car, a yellow Desperado GT, the Gold Medal winner built right here at NJMM. I take a last look at the old factory. I love the red brick and high windows, the Weld shop's dancing robots, the Paint shop's cathedral-like ceilings, the symphonic Assembly shop where everything comes together, and the rail yard out back where each day we release a thousand gleaming and beautiful Desperado sports cars.

Manufacturing is my home. What else am I going to do?

* Japanese for "real place." In manufacturing, *gemba* means the place where value is created (i.e., the factory floor).

Study Questions

1. Everything seems to be going well for Tom. Why do you think he's unhappy?
2. Tom suggests that company culture is like "a set of glasses that filter and often distort reality."
    a. Do you agree or disagree? Explain your answer with examples.
    b. How would you describe your organization's culture? Sketch out your answer using as few written words as possible.* Don't worry if you "can't draw." It's okay to use simple stick figures, circles, and arrows.
3. Tom feels Taylor Motors' "corporate antibodies" awakening.
    a. What do you think he means?
    b. What do corporate antibodies seek to achieve, and how?
    c. Can you give any examples from your experience?

---

* *The Back of the Napkin* by Dan Roam (New York: Penguin 2008) illustrates the power of visual thinking and provides tips on how to get started.

2

The Humpty Dumpty Bar & Grill

I pull onto I-95 and head north toward Queens and my parents' restaurant, where I'm meeting Sarah and the girls for dinner. The Humpty Dumpty Bar & Grill is a joint at the corner of 31st Street and Ditmars Blvd. in the Astoria neighborhood—Greektown. There's a neon sign outside—Humpty taking a header, which for the longest time was a metaphor for my life. Unlike Humpty, I've managed to put my life back together, even if I'm not feeling so hot.

Traffic is moving well. I set my iPod to piano jazz, the Oscar Peterson trio. I've been a blues guitar player all my life, and even had a band for a while. In fact, I met Sarah at one of our gigs. But I've gotten dissatisfied with the guitar and with the blues. It's not the instrument or the genre; it's me.

I'm pushing buttons like crazy, trying to rediscover my kefi. Sarah encouraged me to take up piano and jazz. So on Saturday afternoons I head into the West Village for a lesson with Josh, a good-natured young fellow who studies IT by day and plays gigs by night.

Josh and I are working through the "Great American Songbook." I'm learning songs by Irving Berlin, Duke Ellington, Cole Porter, and others. This week it's "Blues in the Night" by Arlen and Mercer, the best blues song I've ever heard.

I'm struck by the parallels between jazz and my day job. Both are based on standards and connections. In jazz, "standards" include standard scales, chords, and arpeggios. "Connections" comprise the common chord progressions. There's a magnetic attraction, a pull, a yearning, between certain chords. Great songwriters add nuance and feeling in various ways but they're usually combining and riffing on underlying patterns.

Andy has helped me understand the standards and connections in manufacturing, design, and engineering. He smiles when I tell him about the parallels with music. "You are working very hard, Tom-san."

I've also taken up aikido again, the Japanese martial art I studied in my teens and early adulthood. The old dojo is still on West 142nd Street, as is our sensei, Mr. Chiba, Shihan,* a jovial and now white-haired bear still strong and nimble in his seventies. My daughter Sophie is taking aikido with me. My ex-wife, Teal, and I hope her sister will join too.

Aikido is also based on standards and connections. Core standards are known as *kata. Kata connect* to one another in limitless combinations. Chiba-sensei says, "Aikido is endless and eternal." The highest expression of the art is *jiyu waza*, or "free style," which has the quality of jazz improvisation.

Aikido gave me structure and meaning when I was kid. I now realize the Toyota system is also a form of *budo*.† Aikido's core techniques connect to one another, and to one's deeper being. You practice TPS‡ your whole life, the way you practice aikido, judo, or karate. You never achieve perfection, but that's not the point. Commitment to a "way" and daily improvement is the point. Or as Andy says, "every day a little up."

---

* Japanese for "master instructor."

† Japanese for "way of the warrior," or martial art.

‡ Toyota Production System.

Maybe I am a warrior, as Sarah suggests. Can I be a warrior as well as a good husband and father?

I take the Lincoln Tunnel and NY-495 E across Manhattan and into Queens. I get off at the Astoria exit and soon I'm in Greektown. There's Christos Billiards where my Uncle Angie holds court Saturday afternoons. I'm worried about Angie. He has heart trouble and is going into the hospital again. Aunt Jenny has been after him to eat better and give up the ouzo and cigarettes. "We have grandchildren, agape mou."

Angie and Dad ran the Humpty Bar & Grill (Figure 2.1) in the early days. They were always at loggerheads, so Dad bought him out. Angie then embarked on a series of oddball enterprises beginning with Kaboom Rockets—*The Kaboominator Rocket Pack—buy ten and get a free fire extinguisher!* His latest business, Roach Patrol, is also his most successful. "Want to know the secret?" he says, sotto voce. "Don't kill them all."

FIGURE 2.1
The Humpty Dumpty Bar & Grill. Copyright 2015 Lean Pathways Inc.

A new yoga studio, a computer repair place, a new Indian restaurant…There's Holy Name church and Parish Hall where I played stickball with my buddy Dean Formica, now a big shot at Toyota's Kentucky factory. And there's the Humpty Dumpty.

I'm early. I park the car, get out, and stretch a bit after the long drive. My parents, Nick and Noula, have run the place for more than forty years. My brother, Harry, and I worry about them too. It's a tough business and they're starting to slow down. Dad has had heart trouble too and a few years back we almost lost him.

Mama shrugs off our concerns. "What else are we going to do, chriso mou?" Dad has cut back his hours, and Mama has promised to do the same. Uncle Louie can handle it, I tell her.

Harry and I helped out as kids. We cleared tables, delivered sandwiches, and worked the cash register. It was fun, but our parents insisted on a better life for us. Education was sacred. "We don't want you to work like we do."

So I became an engineer and factory manager. My brother Harry is a PhD pharmacologist specializing in oncology—"solid tumors mainly." He leads a team of researchers at a major pharmaceutical firm. I'm blown away by the brilliance of the work. "I wish the *application* of the research was as brilliant," Harry says. He's not enamored of our hospitals.

There's the famous Humpty Dumpty marquee, and the neon GOOD FOOD sign in the window. Years ago, when some of the lights burned out, Mama had a marketing brainwave. "Nicky, come and stand under the sign. I'm going to take your picture. That's it. Now give me a big smile!"

The GOO F photo made Dad Astoria royalty and the Humpty Dumpty a local landmark. The walls are covered with celebrity photographs. Tony Bennett mugging with Mama, Mike Tyson mixing it up with Dad, Telly Savalas putting a headlock on Uncle Louie.

I walk through the front door. It's busy for a Wednesday night. The long Formica counter with the spin-around stools is full, as are most of the tables. Uncle Louie is working the cash register. Waiters and waitresses pick up their orders at the serving window. I catch glimpses of Mama and Dad in the kitchen. Dad is wearing his chef's hat, Mama a white kerchief. Sarah and the girls haven't arrived yet.

Uncle Louie sees me and waves. He hollers through the serving window. "Tommy's here!" Dad is cooking something. Mama comes out of the kitchen drying her hands. She embraces me and leads me to a table by the long front window. "Sarah and the girls?" "On their way."

"I have to help your father in the kitchen," she says. "Spiros will take care of you. We'll sit with you as soon as we can. By the way, your brother is going to drop in."

A few minutes later Sarah, Sophie, and Helen arrive. Helen is thirteen, Sophie "almost twelve." Only yesterday, they were curly-haired munchkins. Spiros pours Sarah and me a Santorini white and brings Shirley Temples for the girls.

"Sorry we're late," says Sarah. "Traffic."

"How was your day, Dad?" Helen asks. She's a nice kid, thoughtful and more serious than her jitterbug sister.

"It was a good day, my dear. We had our monthly status meeting, then walked the factory."

"We had a dance rehearsal," Sophie says. "You're coming to the show, right?"

"We'll be there," says Sarah.

Spiros brings out feta cheese and olives and takes our orders. "The dolmades are amazing," he tells me. When the dinner rush is over, Mama and Dad come over and sit with us. They watch us have dinner. We've eaten, they say. Spiros brings out the dessert tray, just as Harry arrives.

"LOOK AT THIS—THE PAPAS TABLE!" Dad hollers. "THERE'S NOTHING LIKE FAMILY!"

"That voice of yours, Niko," Mama says, "they can hear you on Broadway!"

"I GOT A BIG VOICE, AND A BIG NOSE! I'M LIKE WHAT'S HIS NAME—CYRIANO!"

"Pappou, you're too funny," says Sophie. "You mean Cyrano de Bergerac."

"DE WHAT? I THOUGHT HE WAS GREEK! YOU KNOW, TELLY SAVALAS ONCE PLAYED CYRIANO. I MISS TELLY. HE WAS THE BEST GRAND MARSHAL THE GREEK PARADE HAS EVER HAD. TELLY WAS AN ASTORIA BOY, YOU KNOW."

Pappou is in full flow. Look at him, I thought. Mr. Kefi. Almost seventy-five, and still full of beans.

My brother and I catch up. One of Harry's research projects is in trouble. "HNYC has messed up. Please keep it confidential."

"Of course. What's HNYC?"

"Hospitals of New York City—they run all the public hospitals and clinics in the five boroughs. They've messed up our drug trials. Wrong drugs, wrong doses, wrong patients."

I knew enough about my brother's work to grasp the implications. Advanced chemotherapy entails administering a cocktail of highly toxic drugs specific to the patient, his or her tumor, and genetics. "Wrong drug, wrong dose, wrong patient" means people could die.

"Mana mou."

"It gets worse," says Harry. "It's not just drug trials; the same problems may exist in drug *therapy*. If so, it's going to be all over the papers."

I can't believe what I'm hearing.

Just then Uncle Angie himself bursts through the door. He sees us and saunters over, "Spiro," he hollers, "a bottle of moschofilero for the table! How is everybody?"

"We're good, Angie," says Harry. "How are you feeling these days?"

Angie sinks into a chair like an emperor settling into a warm bath. "To tell the truth," he says, "I've been better." He taps his chest. "This ticker of mine…"

"Don't you worry, chriso mou," Mama says. "The doctors are going to fix your heart. You're going to be just like new."

"I hope so, Noula," Angie says. "I don't like feeling like this."

Study Questions

1. Tom suggests there are commonalities between the Toyota Production System (Lean) and music.
   a. Do you agree or disagree?
   b. Explain your answer.
2. Tom also suggests there are commonalities between the TPS and the martial arts.
   a. Do you agree or disagree?
   b. Explain your answer.
3. Tom's brother, Harry, describes serious errors in a research hospital pharmacy ("wrong drug, wrong dose, wrong patient").
   a. Is this realistic? Explain your answer.
   b. Provide at least one scenario whereby such errors could occur.
   c. In your chosen scenario(s), what are the root causes of the problem?
   d. What are possible countermeasures?

3

Rachel and Gwendolyn

Rachel Armstrong is from Pittsburgh. Her Dad had been an hourly worker at the famous Homestead Works, U.S. Steel's flagship plant. She was the only one of four children to go to college. It was a fluke, Rachel said. Her parents couldn't afford tuition fees. But one day Rachel read an ad in the paper. Carnegie Mellon University was offering free scholarships to qualified students who could write an essay explaining why they wanted to go to college. Rachel won the scholarship and was on her way.

Rachel is close to her family and loves her hometown. A few years back she asked me to join her on a cross-continent "go-see" of several factories. We took the company jet and, on the way back, stopped in Pittsburgh. Her parents were waiting on the tarmac—humble people who'd lived a hard life, like my folks. After introductions, Rachel invited her folks on to the jet for a tour. They were proud and somewhat in awe of their daughter. Rachel's mother told us she'd never been on a jet plane before.

Rachel called me from her office in Taylor City, Michigan. "I'm in New York City next week. I'd like you to join me for a meeting."

"Of course," I said. "Who and where?"

"Hospitals of New York City, lower Manhattan."

"HNYC? What do we have to talk about?"

"An unusual proposition. I'll meet you there."

* *

I'm walking north on Broadway toward HNYC headquarters near City Hall Park, always nice in autumn. City Hall and the Court House come into view, then the fountain and Municipal Building. Way up on the pinnacle, I can just make out the statue of "Civic Fame," who looks like Liberty's little sister.

Rachel hasn't said a word. All I know is, we're meeting senior HNYC officials to "talk about how we might work together." Last time something like this happened, she offered me the shusa* job, for which I was wholly unqualified.†

"HNYC is a monster," Harry told me. My research bore him out: One of America's biggest municipal healthcare systems, 30,000 employees, $9 billion in revenue, 14 major hospitals and dozens of clinics and related services, more than a million patients served including almost 400,000 noninsured patients. Harry and I were born in an HNYC hospital, as were Sophie and Helen.

HNYC's flagship is Grandview, one of the nation's oldest public hospitals, founded in 1752. The iconic and somewhat creepy brown brick buildings overlook the East River, just a short cab ride a way. The Psychiatric Hospital's old wrought iron gate has appeared in a number of horror movies. The adjoining fence encloses grounds that, though lush in spring and summer, turn sinister in winter. A few years back Sarah and I saw a disturbing

* "Chief engineer."

† Chapter 2 of *The Remedy: Bringing Lean Out of the Factory to Transform the Entire Organization* (Hoboken, NJ: John Wiley & Sons, 2010).

documentary about old asylums in which Grandview was prominent.

I make my way to HNYC headquarters, a blocky ten-story building with a white granite façade. Not exactly ugly, but a letdown after City Hall Park. Like most healthcare providers, HNYC is in the midst of a fiscal storm, which has driven them into a deep deficit. Increasingly, they are getting paid based on outcomes and not on activity. Patient readmissions, for example, which generated revenue in the past, now trigger penalties. It's only going to get worse.

Flat revenue and rising cost—welcome to the real world. HNYC has responded with the usual tired drill—staff cuts of almost 10 percent, reorganization, and "service consolidation." Despite the cuts, they still have a structural deficit of almost half a billion dollars. HNYC has to increase revenue and find a better way of reducing costs.

A few years ago, HNYC faced a literal storm. Hurricane Sandy shut down several facilities for weeks. Staff worked heroically and patients were protected, but they've still not recovered from the staggering revenue loss and cleanup cost. HNYC is always in the media, a political football to be kicked whenever it suits a politico.

I walk into a marble foyer. After a brief chat with security, I take the elevator to the Executive Suite. The door opens to a striking reception area—leather chairs and couches, large windows, and a panoramic view of New York.

"We've been expecting you," they tell me. "Ms. Armstrong is already here." A young fellow escorts me to a meeting room. Help yourself to coffee, he says. I do.

I hear a sing-song somewhat Caribbean voice, along with Rachel's (Figure 3.1). A smiling matronly woman with chocolate skin and black glasses walks in. In tow is Rachel, who makes the introductions. "Hi Tom. I'd like you to meet

FIGURE 3.1
Rachel and Gwendolyn. Copyright 2015 Lean Pathways Inc.

Gwendolyn Carter, president and CEO of Hospitals of New York City."

"Please call me Gwen. So good to meet you. Welcome to HNYC."

"Tom is one of our most innovative leaders," Rachel says. "His factories are the best in the Taylor System. Every year they produce better quality at lower cost, without firing people. In fact, Tom's factories are hiring."

"Better quality and lower cost," Gwen says, "that's what we need at HNYC. I've been CEO only for six months, but it's the same story at each facility. My senior executives tell me it's impossible."

"It's a hard road," I say, "You have to keep surfacing problems. It's humbling."

"Humility is not our strong suit," says Gwen Carter.

"I grew up in a Greek restaurant," I tell them. "That's as humble as it gets."

"A restaurant rat—me too!" says Gwen. "I grew up in a fish joint in Georgetown, Grand Cayman. My Dad died young so it was Mama and three girls running a diner. Mama ran it for thirty years and put us all through college. She passed a few years ago."

Gwen pauses, her eyes glistening. I catch a glimmer of the character that has propelled her from a small Caymanian diner to the top of HNYC.

Gwen describes the chessboard that is NYC healthcare. It's a multidimensional board extending into municipal, state, and national politics. The board is often foggy and there are multiple competing armies (Figure 3.2). But the main question remains unanswered. *Why are we here?*

Rachel reads my mind. "Gwen and I are old friends. She knows all about Taylor Motors' transformation, about NJMM and the rest."

FIGURE 3.2
The challenges facing HNYC. Copyright 2015 Lean Pathways Inc.

"When I accepted the CEO position," Gwen says, "I knew it would be hard. But things are worse than I expected. We have to manage in a different way. Otherwise, we're facing a long slow decline ending in bankruptcy."

"Gwen has asked Taylor Motors to help HNYC improve safety, quality, delivery, and cost," says Rachel, "and we've agreed. Toyota has been working with NYC food banks to great effect. Why shouldn't we help too? For a start, we're going to offer pro bono training at your NJMM Lean Learning Center. But we need a practical example too, a learning laboratory where HNYC folks can learn by doing."

I didn't like where this was going.

Gwen spoke softly. "Tom, I'm inviting you to join HNYC on a two-year assignment. You'll be a senior level executive at a major hospital, with a dotted line relationship to me. Your assignment will be to do there what you did at New Jersey Motor Manufacturing, and with the Chloe platform. You'll have everything you need to do the job, I promise you. As for salary, just give us a number. Rachel has generously offered to split the cost."

"High-profile assignment," Rachel adds. "The Taylor Motors board, the mayor and governor are with us. When you come back, you can write your own ticket. Joe Grace would handle your Domo responsibilities. You and I know he'd do a good job."

I look out the window. Cars inching along Broadway, people walking around City Hall Park. I feel all my old wounds. I think of Sarah, Sophie, and Helen, and my folks. All the people who need me, and who I've at times neglected in my compulsive rush for achievement. I think of Andy Saito, my sensei and friend, living alone in Essex Fells.

"I can't do it," I tell them. "It's too much. I have to look after my family."

"I understand Tom," Rachel says. "But please think about it. There are a lot of positives. You'd take the subway to work. There'd be no corporate travel. I'll bet you'd have *more* time with your family, not less. You'd get to apply all you've learned in a brand new field."

"You'd be doing our city and the country a great service," Gwen says. "Healthcare has to make the journey the automotive industry has made. If not, it could bankrupt us."

"I understand that," I tell them. "But I'm not sure I have enough gas in the tank. Besides, I'm unqualified. What do I know about healthcare?"

"That might be an advantage," says Gwen. "We need fresh eyes, someone who can see all the waste without preconceptions. We also need someone with a record of achievement. Our people are smart and some are arrogant. To command their attention, we need a heavyweight."

"It's like the Chloe launch,* Tom," Rachel says. "You didn't know much about design or marketing, or about our supply

---

* Described in *The Remedy: Bringing Lean Out of the Factory to Transform the Entire Organization* (Hoboken, NJ: John Wiley & Sons, 2010).

chain and dealer network. But you built a good team and a good system. You all figured it out together, and in the end we had a fine launch. I'm betting you can do the same with a large hospital. And you won't be alone. I've already talked to Andy Saito. He said he has talk to you first, but sounds like he's open to it."

That gets my attention. It would be great to work with Andy again. I like Gwen and sense a kindred spirit. Harry has a deep knowledge of HNYC and of healthcare in general and would be a great resource. And the thought of taking the subway to work and no corporate travel is appealing. Surely there's no harm in deferring a decision till I've talked to my family.

"What's the pilot hospital?"

"Grandview," Gwen says.

* *

"I'm okay with it," said Sarah. "It actually sounds pretty good—subway to work, home each night for dinner." We were sitting on our balcony, looking out over the Hudson River. Ferries and tugboats were churning by.

"I'd be pulling some late hours," I said.

"I know, but you'll be a subway ride away. No more flights to Michigan or Ohio, or to suppliers all over the world. We'll be able to see more of Sophie and Helen too."

Unspoken was our unfinished conversation. *Would we have children?* If I took a killer assignment, would I have the energy to help Sarah?

"I don't want to get sucked into another hurricane," I said. "I want to be here."

"I know that."

Sophie and Helen were impressed. "Daddy, that's so cool," Helen said. "Can we get a tour of the hospital? I want to see a surgery."

"No way," said Sophie, "I hate the sight of blood."

* *

Harry, normally circumspect, is brutally candid. "Healthcare, in general, and Grandview in particular, are a disaster. The people are dedicated, but the leadership and management system are all over the place. I know changing Taylor Motors culture has been tough. But the worst Taylor factory is better managed than the best hospital in America. In fact, there's no comparison. Taylor Motors competes with the world's best companies and has been working at continuous improvement for decades. Things you take for granted at NJMM are entirely missing in healthcare."

"Hold on, Harry," I tell him. "How can things be *that* bad? Every week we hear about a new medical miracle."

"I call it the Great Paradox," Harry says. "Miracles happen *within* the silos, and disaster across them."

"HNYC has been dabbling with Lean," he continues, "which they call 'Breakout.' I hear Grandview has a good Breakout team, but I doubt they've gained traction. Many healthcare people don't want to change. They're smart and stubborn and they'll wait you out."

How can miracles and disaster coexist in the same management system?

"Harry, do I really want this job?"

"I'd give them a list of conditions," he answers. "For a start, Andy Saito has to be there. Here are some other ideas:

1. Several of your top factory people come with you to Grandview.

2. Your position, whatever they call it, is equal to that of the chief operating officer.
3. You have an adequate budget to cover important kaizen* including adding people if need be.
4. You have a direct link to HNYC's CEO—a help chain as it were.
5. You have the prerogative of walking away and returning to Taylor Motors at your discretion.

The help chain is really important. People have to know that you're Gwen Carter's eyes and ears. I can coach you on healthcare fundamentals—the lines of care, technology, and mindsets. My pharma team keeps an office near Grandview."

My parents are supportive, as always.

"WHEN TOMMY PUTS HIS MIND TO SOMETHING," Dad bellows, "THERE'S NOTHING HE CANNOT DO! AND YOU KNOW WHY? BECAUSE YOU, MY BOY, ARE A PHENOMENA!"

"Phenomena," spelled with an "A," was a Nick Papas' trademark.

"We're going to have to wear ear plugs, Nicky," says Mama. "Your Dad's right, agape mou. If you put your mind to it, you can do it. I'm glad you won't be traveling as much. I don't like all those airplanes. I only worry about too many late hours. Sarah is a wonderful girl and she deserves children."

Andy Saito was in Japan when we spoke. "I would enjoy working together again, Tom-san. If you accept, I will join you. But before accepting, you must grasp the situation."

We agree to meet at the Japanese Cultural Center in Jersey City when he returns from Japan. We'll have an aikido class followed by lunch.

* Japanese for "to take apart and put back together"; continuous improvement.

I take an afternoon off to scout out Grandview. I walk through the famous arches and into the new atrium. They've just completed a major renovation. Light pours in through the sloped skylight onto the brick façade and new curved balconies above.

I wander over to the Cancer Center. What do I see? People sitting in a room waiting to be called to one of five registration windows. The clerks are frequently interrupted by hospital staff.

"My wife and I have been waiting half an hour," an older man tells me. The woman next to him shakes her head. "Wait till you go to Phlebotomy."

"Why does registration take so long?" I ask a nurse.

"New software," she replies.

"But shouldn't that make registration quicker?" I ask.

"It would," she says, "if they bothered to talk to us before installing it."

"How come the clerks keep getting interrupted?"

She shrugs, "It's usually people looking for information or making some kind of change."

I walk over to Phlebotomy and see more of the same. Four registration windows and a waiting room full of people. "How long have you been here?" I ask an elderly woman. "Over an hour," she says. "My husband just went in there. They're taking his blood."

As in the Cancer Center, Phlebotomy registration staff keep getting interrupted. I wonder what's happening behind the wall. Are there also interruptions during blood draws, labeling, and analysis? How good are the process standards? Is defect-proofing built into them? How good are connections between the silos?

I begin to understand how "wrong drug, wrong dose, wrong patient" might happen. I return to the main lobby and order espresso at the open air café. I take in the atrium, façade, and all the people hurrying by. It might as well be Oz.

Do I really want to do this? Am I falling into the same old trap—taking on a great challenge, a desperate fight to mask a deeper discontent? I know how to fight. Do I know how to live my life?

* *

"What do you think of Tommy's new job offer, my dear?" Noula asked.

"It sounds good," Sarah replied.

"I worry," said Noula. "Tommy works so hard. I want him to slow down and enjoy life more."

"I worry too, Noula. But Tom's becoming more self-aware. I think it's going to be okay."

"Tommy's suffered a lot," Noula said. "Every day I pray to St. Spyridon, and I thank him that you and Tommy found each other."

Study Questions

1. Is "better quality with lower cost" possible? Explain your answer with practical examples.
    a. Can you think of other industries that are facing intense pressure to provide better quality at lower cost?
    b. What are these industries doing about it? How effective are these measures?
    c. Can you suggest any reflections or learning points?
2. Tom's brother Harry suggests "many healthcare people don't want to change."
    a. Do you agree or disagree? Explain your answer with practical examples.
    b. Can you think of any other industries where this is (or was) true? What's happening in these industries now? Can you suggest any learning points?

3. Harry also describes the "Great Paradox" in healthcare—miracles within the silos, and disaster across them.
   a. Do you agree or disagree with Harry's point of view?
   b. Explain your answer.
4. Can a revolutionary idea in one field, for example, TPS in auto manufacturing, migrate effectively to a totally different field? Explain your answer.
   a. What has to happen for the migration to be effective?
   b. Can you provide any examples from your personal experience?
   c. What are the biggest obstacles to such "lateral learning"?
   d. What are possible countermeasures to these obstacles?

4

My Uncle's Funeral

"Angie's gone," said Harry.

I look at my cell phone. Cars are coming into Final Inspection. Team members are doing quality checks. It's very bright in here. "You okay, Tom?" someone hollers.

"Early this morning," said Harry. "He died early this morning."

Last month Angie went into Queens General Hospital, an HNYC site, for a "routine" coronary bypass. Three weeks later he's gone.

* *

We follow the hearse from St. Irene's Greek Orthodox Cathedral to Pineview Cemetery, to that little bit of Greece in section 26: Stavridis, Stratas, Axiotis. "Me too, one day," says Mama, red-eyed. She has been up all night, crying softly and swaying her head back and forth like people from the old country do.

Memories… Saturday afternoons at Christos Billiards, Angie holding court. "Shape," he'd crow, "just look at that shape!" as the crowd gathered. "So this cab driver says to his doctor, 'How come my keister hurts so much?' And the doctor says…"

It's cloudy and cool. Angie didn't like autumn. I feel sluggish. Harry and I help our folks out of the limousine. Uncle Louie puts his hand on my shoulder, "Angie, he made me laugh so hard once, I actually wet my pants."

Angie's last days were bleak. The charge nurse claimed there was no linen, so Angie had to wear a diaper. He passed away at 4:00 in the morning. Aunt Jennie was there alone and asked the hospital not to take the body away till her boys Billy and George arrived.

But Jennie nodded off and when she woke Angie's body was gone. After an hour of grief and rage the hospital retrieved the body and put it in a basement storage room, which is where Jenny and the boys said goodbye.

Aunt Toula has brought spanakopita, feta cheese, and Kalamata olives, which she lays out on tables near the gravesite, in accord with Greek tradition. Uncle Jimmy lays out bottles of wine, ouzo, and Metaxa brandy.

I walk over to Harry, who is having a hard time.

"Remember Angie's haiku?" he asks.

I nod. Harry and I used to get pleasure from turning Angie's musings into Japanese poetry.

"I wrote some of them down," Harry says.

He takes out a notebook and starts reading:

Uncle Angie's Haiku

Fresh

Is the OJ fresh?
"*Yup,*" she tells me.
"It's still got ice crystals in it."

On the iPhone

A tool used by muck-ups
To explain
How they mucked up.

On Sushi
Hold the rice
Seaweed & raw fish
And I'm okay with it.

We're both laughing and our eyes are wet.

Father Stephanos arrives and directs Harry and me and the other pallbearers to carry the coffin to the gravesite. Father Stephanos recites the short Trisagion prayer in Greek and English and bestows his final blessing. Angie's kids and grandkids gather around Aunt Jenny and watch as the coffin goes down. We toss in flowers. Harry tosses in haiku. Your jokes, your pranks, your goofball grin, where are they now, poor Angie (Figure 4.1)?

FIGURE 4.1
Uncle Angie's funeral. Copyright 2015 Lean Pathways Inc.

Harry and I make our way to Aunt Jennie and the family. Her boys, Billy and George, are holding her up. "Sillipiteria, thea. We loved him."

"Zoe se mas," she says. "I loved him too."

Aunt Toula is filling paper plates with meze. Uncle Jimmy is pouring shots. Harry and I knock back a brandy.

"Never thought a heart attack could take Angie down," I tell him.

"It wasn't a heart attack."

"What do you mean?"

"It wasn't a heart attack," Harry says. "It was a CLABSI. Central-line associated bloodstream infection. Happens so often they have an acronym."

"Angie died of an infection?"

Harry nods. "That's what my spies tell me. An avoidable infection. Imagine that, after all the indignities."

"Why don't we sue the bastards?"

"I thought about it," says Harry. "But it just seems like more stress, and what's the chance of winning?"

I look over at Aunt Jennie. How will she manage? Billy and George look lost. The grandkids are confused. Where is our Pappou?

* *

The next few weeks are a blur. I talk to Sarah, Andy, and Harry some more, trying to weigh the implications of taking on Grandview Hospital. Finally, I call Gwen and Rachel and tell them I'm in. Okay, they reply, tell us what you need. I call Andy and he signs on too.

I'm scared. I think I can do some good. But Grandview is a monster that might devour me.

Study Questions

1. How many people die of medical errors (including infections and mis-medications) in American hospitals each year? (Non-American readers, please answer the question for your country as well.)
   a. Describe at least one such case, either from your personal experience or from your reading.
   b. What was the root cause of the incident?
   c. What countermeasures were applied and how effective do you think they were? Explain your answer.
2. Is such information readily available and widely publicized in America? (Non-American readers, please answer the question for your country as well.)
   a. Explain your answer.
3. Medical errors "kill enough people to fill four jumbo jets a week."* Yet they go largely unnoticed by the public and the medical community. By contrast, plane crashes, though very rare, make headlines and trigger thorough accident investigations, whose lessons are broadly shared across the aviation industry.
   a. Explain the paradox.
   b. What would need to happen to change the situation?

* "How to Stop Hospitals from Killing Us," by Marty Makary, *Harvard Business Review* September 2012, p. 1.

5

Andy Saito

I turn off Christopher Columbus Boulevard and into the Japanese Cultural Center. Andy and I are to take an aikido class, then discuss Grandview over lunch. I park and pull my aikido bag out of the back seat—*gi*,* *zoris*,† and navy blue *hakama*.‡ Aikido's values or standards are those of *bushido*§ and are expressed in the seven folds of the *hakama*.¶ Standards are also central to Andy's teaching and the foundation of the famous Toyota Production System (TPS; Figure 5.1).

Toyota's problems over the past five years have pained Andy and show how tough it is to sustain TPS. Andy believes Toyota has grown too fast, faster than its ability to teach TPS. He's encouraged that Toyota accepted responsibility for the quality and safety problems and didn't scapegoat its supplier. There was much reflection in Toyoda City, Andy told me, including

* A lightweight two-piece white garment worn in the martial arts, typically comprising loose-fitting pants and a jacket that is closed with a cloth belt.

† A Japanese sandal, often made of straw or rubber and consisting of a flat sole held on the foot by a thong passing between the first and second toes.

‡ Traditional Japanese pleated trousers.

§ The code of honor and morals developed by the samurai.

¶ The seven folds in the *hakama*, five in the front, two in the back, represent the seven virtues of *bushido*: *Yuki* = courage; *Jin* = charity; *Gi* = justice; *Rei* = courtesy; *Makoto* = honesty; *Chugi* = fidelity; *Meiyo* = honor.

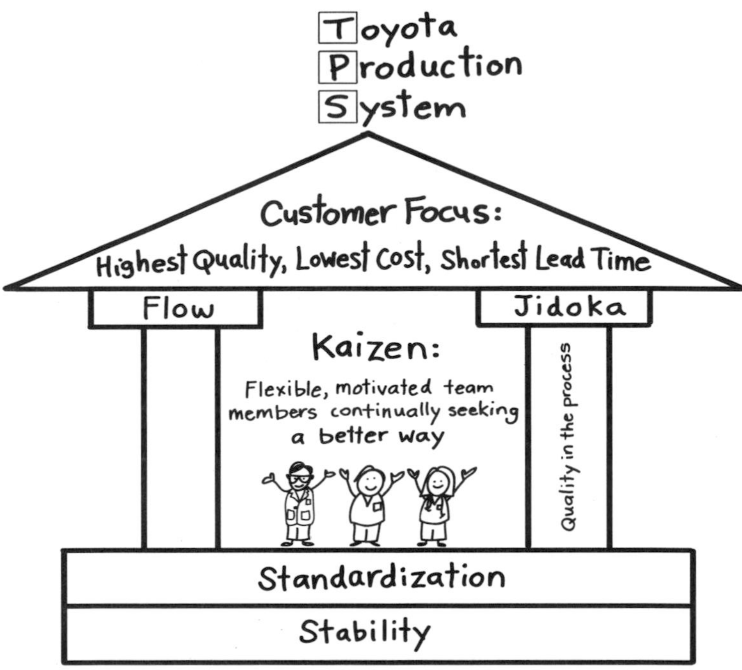

FIGURE 5.1
Toyota Production System. Copyright 2015 Lean Pathways Inc.

hansei, the sincere acknowledgment of failure and the commitment to improve. Over the past decade Toyota has lost a ton of talent. There was only one countermeasure: grow more senseis.

I walk up the steps, past reception, and into the men's change room. It's Saturday and the children's class is just finishing. I change quickly, bow, and step onto the tatami mat. It's a big class, maybe forty people.

Andy, with his silver hair, moustache, and little boy grin, is doing light stretches. When he sees me, he makes a droll face. "Oh, my aching shoulders." A few minutes later, the sensei claps, we bow to the portrait of Morehei Ueshiba, O'Sensei, and the class begins.

Andy and I practice a few techniques together. He's exceptionally strong and fluid for his age. After class, I'm sweaty and sore, but feel great. The Japanese call it *Ki*, which means life force, energy, heart, and "spirit of movement." "When your body makes good movements, it feels good!" Chiba-sensei likes to say.

Ki suggests the Western concept of *Flow*—complete absorption and enjoyment in the process of what you're doing. At times you're so engrossed in the technique, you can lose yourself. *Mushin*, the Japanese call it—"no mind."

We decide on McSorley's for lunch and head to the Hoboken waterfront. We take a table near the water and order lunch, lingering over the bourbon menu. I go with Four Roses, on the rocks with a twist of lime. Andy decides on Basel Hayden, neat. We click glasses.

"Kampai, Tom-san. Thank you for your kind invitation."

"I'm honored, sensei. Thank you for joining the team."

Andy tells me about his Japan trip. His daughters are well. Japan's economy is showing signs of life, although Andy's not sure about President Abe's foreign policy. Toyota is regaining its mojo. I tell him about my family, Uncle Angie's death, and the latest Taylor Motors scuttlebutt.

After lunch, I fire up my iPad and take Andy through my Grandview research. Gwen Carter has opened the information vault, and there's also a ton on the Internet. Andy listens quietly.

- 4200 full-time employees
- 730 beds
- 215 psychiatric beds
- 27,492 discharges per year (75 per day)

- Average length of stay
    - Acute care: 5.4 days
    - Psychiatry: 15.8 days
    - Rehabilitation: 18.6 days
- Clinic visits
    - Emergency room: 105,402 (289 per day)
    - Non-emergency room: 482,629 (1322 per day)
    - Total primary care: 107,296 (294 per day)
    - Total psychiatric: 40,520 (111 per day)
    - Total physical medicine: 15,382 (42 per day)
    - Total methadone and chemical dependency: 59,302 (162 per day)

Grandview's primary service area comprises almost two million people, 36 percent of whom are considered "safety net" patients, meaning they're either uninsured or covered by Medicaid. They're disproportionately young and poor. Almost 25 percent of individuals and 34 percent of families have incomes below the poverty line. English is a second language for almost two thirds, Spanish and Chinese being the most common first languages. Their biggest health problems include asthma, hypertension, obesity, diabetes, cancer, substance abuse, and depression and other forms of mental illness (Figure 5.2).

Is the healthcare industry in touch with patients? All of the literature refers to the "Three Ps": Patient, Provider, and Payer. Do the needs of the latter two, doctors and insurers, always align with those of the patients? Harry says there's a fourth player, the facility, whose different pay models can create widely differing incentive structures.

In the auto industry there's no such ambiguity. J.D. Power and others provide detailed feedback on clear and shared industry metrics. We know where the shoe pinches. A few years

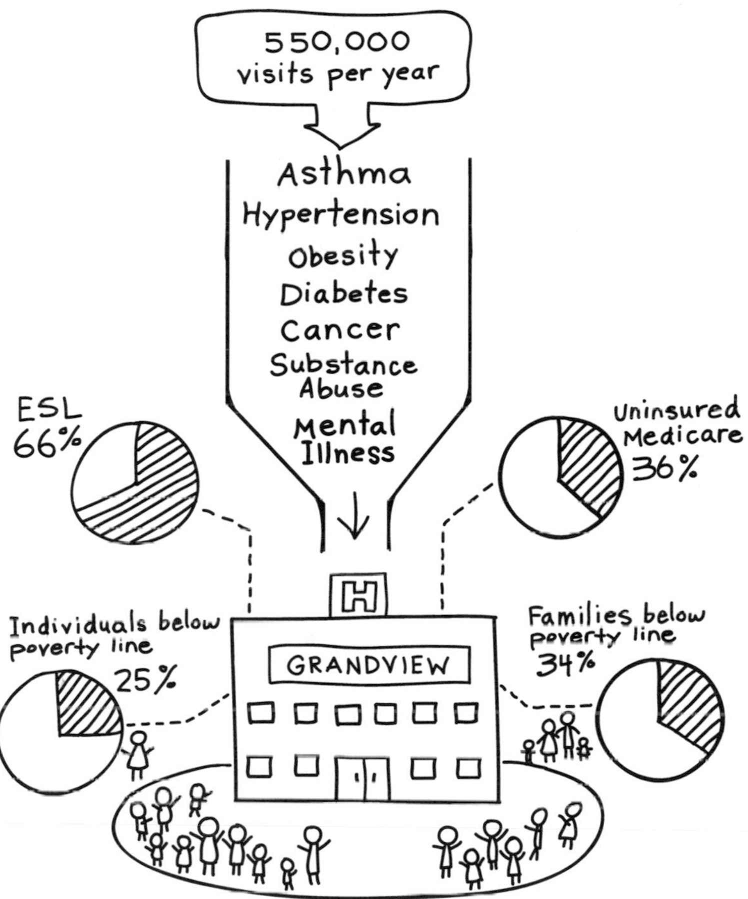

FIGURE 5.2
Grandview Hospital. Copyright 2015 Lean Pathways Inc.

ago, for example, Desperado customers told us they wanted a quieter ride. We translated the customer's voice into discrete decibel targets, which triggered design, engineering, and manufacturing improvements. Result: less cab noise and vibration. Similar work on other hotspots helped us win the J.D. Power Gold Medal against tough competition.

I like Grandview's purpose, which we call "True North": "To provide high quality healthcare to all, regardless of their ability to pay." It's a noble goal I can get behind. It takes courage—Grandview takes an annual hit of almost $140 million in uncompensated care.

Grandview's financial analyses are sophisticated and provide a clear picture of the current condition. Here are the most important measures of profitability and liquidity:

- Total annual revenue of almost $1.2 billion
- Net operating loss of $66 million
- Operating deficit of 5.5 percent
- Days of cash on hand, down to 36 days

There are no discernible targets for these, but clearly Grandview is losing the Revenue and Cost game.

How about the Safety, Quality, and Delivery game? I have no idea. A thick fog covers the scoreboard. I'm not even sure what these concepts mean in healthcare. The data largely comprise murky metrics and general surveys. Simple process metrics, the signposts to improvement, are sparse.

"Manage S, Q, and D—and Profitability takes care of itself," Andy says. Grandview seems to have it backwards. To be fair, their cost problems are daunting. The Patient Protection and Affordable Care Act (aka Obamacare) greatly increased the number of people Grandview looks after. Will revenue increase proportionately? There are also painful one-time hits, such as Hurricane Sandy, which resulted in $60 million in lost revenue and substantial uncompensated clean-up costs.

Andy and I watch online videos and some very old photos. We study customer feedback pages. Some people love Grandview, but they're a minority. A few are visceral in their contempt. Have they lost family? I turn off my iPad. We order more bourbon.

"Good summary. Thank you, Tom-san. We will need help."

I take a sip of bourbon. "Gwen and Rachel have agreed to the following:

1. Four Taylor Motors senior senseis will join us and supplement Grandview's internal kaizen team: Becky Johnson, Antonio Villarreal, Elaine Miyazaki, and Benny Walton.
2. My position will be chief process officer, reporting to Gwen Carter, with a dotted line to Dr. Fox, Grandview's CEO. You'll be our special advisor.
3. A discretionary budget will be available to cover important kaizen* activity including adding people in pilot zones, if need be.
4. I will have the prerogative of walking away and returning to Taylor Motors with thirty days' notice.

"Am I missing anything, sensei?"

"List is okay," Andy says. "We have a big challenge. Healthcare leaders have learned to think in a certain way over many years. How will we change their thinking?"

Study Questions

1. The past five years have been difficult for Toyota.
   a. How has Toyota responded to the crisis? Can you suggest any reflections or learning points?
   b. What are the root causes of Toyota's difficulties?
   c. What are the correct countermeasures?
   d. What countermeasures has Toyota taken? Do you think they will be effective? Explain your answers.

---

* Japanese for "to take apart and put back together"; continuous improvement.

2. “Manage S, Q, and D and Profitability takes care of itself.”
   a. Do you agree or disagree? Explain your answer.
   b. Is better S, Q, and D at lower cost possible? Explain your answer.
   c. Provide at least three examples of organizations that have managed to do this. Can you suggest any reflections or learning points?
3. Andy poses a difficult question: “Healthcare leaders have learned to think in a certain way over many years. How will we change their thinking?”
   a. What are some of the core mental models in healthcare?
   b. How do such mental models develop?
   c. How do you change mental models?

6

The Usual Suspects

It's Monday morning. Andy and I take the elevator up to the Grandview executive offices. Gwen Carter is waiting for us. "Let's go meet your new colleagues," she tells us.

Dr. Robert Fox, CEO, is a kindly, soft-spoken Englishman who, Gwen says, is retiring in a few years. Dr. Fox had been a family practitioner with a legendary bedside manner. Late into his career, he still made house calls. He was so good with people that he became head of a major clinic and just kept going.

"Please call me Bob," he said. "I've read a great deal about the Toyota system. I have no doubt it applies in healthcare. I'm focused externally—donors, the mayor's office, the media, and so on. Dr. Harper, who I think you're meeting next, is focused internally and runs the show here. But I'm eager to learn and to help."

Dr. Madeleine Harper, the chief operating officer, is a neurologist and Harvard MBA. She isn't happy to see us and I can't blame her. All of these problems are happening on her watch and here's the new boss with a couple of manufacturing bozos. "Full disclosure, I'm a skeptic, Tom. Healthcare is much more complex than auto manufacturing. We're dealing with people, not with inanimate objects. But I'm open to persuasion. We certainly have to try something."

"Auto manufacturing is about people too," Andy says. "The most important thing is total involvement. How can we engage all team members in improvement work?"

"I've read about total involvement," Dr. Harper replies, "but I'm not convinced. I believe in excellence—extraordinary people, doing extraordinary things. A team of experts who solve the insoluble problems so the front line can do its work."

Dr. Harper was plainly impatient with people or ideas she considered to be second rate. I knew the type. Could we channel her intelligence and hostility into the challenge at hand?

"We believe in excellence too," Andy says, "but our approach is different. We want *ordinary* people doing extraordinary things through strong processes. With respect, Dr. Harper-san, your way is maybe okay in a small research or design team. But does it work in a large hospital? If we do not engage the front line, the people who know the work best, how can we improve?"

Dr. Harper was not used to being challenged. "We believe in empowering our front line," she replies. "We don't interfere with how they do their work. 'It's your show', I tell our charge nurses."

I decide not to push it.

"In any event," she continues, "we have a big challenge ahead. And please call me Madeleine."

Dr. Bill McKnight is chief medical officer, a rangy, goateed Canadian. He's also head of the Emergency Department (ED). "An unusual combination, no?" I offer.

He nods. "ED docs aren't usually top of the totem pole. For some reason, Dr. Fox kicked me up here. I love being an ED doc. You never know what you've got. You have to be like Sherlock Holmes."

"Can we go see the ED together?" I ask Dr. McKnight. "That would be good," he replies.

I turn to follow Gwen, and standing there, grinning like a game show host, is Dr. Zac Brewster, the celebrity surgeon

(Figure 6.1). There's a big scary-looking guy with him. Brewster sticks out his hand. "You must be Gwen Carter."

"Yes, I am," says Gwen, eyeing the big guy. "Good to meet you, Dr. Brewster. I've heard a lot about you."

"Thank you. This is my personal assistant, Lester. Thought I'd say hello. I'm here to see Dr. McKnight."

"We're just finishing up," says McKnight, looking uncomfortable. "I'll see you in my office in a few minutes."

Brewster is "surgeon to the stars" and has his own talk show. Turns out he's a visiting surgeon here. Dr. Brewster oozes charm, arrogance, and power. He barely acknowledges Andy and me. Lester glowers at us. Gwen extricates herself and we continue our tour.

Carol Kwan, chief nursing officer, is a firecracker with straight black hair and a big smile. "Nurses are the backbone of this organization," she tells us.

FIGURE 6.1
Dr. Brewster, surgeon to the stars. Copyright 2015 Lean Pathways Inc.

"We have four nurses in our New Jersey factory's Health Center," I tell her. "They've really taken to Toyota fundamentals."

"Not surprised," Carol says. "Nurses understand the importance of standards. On a given shift you might do 50 or 60 different things. We even have our own version of Plan–Do–Check–Adjust. Our problem is lack of support. Dr. Harper doesn't want to hear it, but indiscriminate staffing cuts are killing us."

"Can you explain, Carol-san?"

"Did Dr. Harper tell you about 'empowerment'? Thought so. You know what empowerment really means? *Abandonment.* We've lost many of our charge nurses, and almost all of our assistant nursing managers. Our span of control is ridiculous. Let's schedule some time together. I've got a lot to show you."

Arnold Penniman, the chief financial officer, is a burly African American from Philly. His office is full of Eagles memorabilia. Like Dr. Harper, he's an Ivy League MBA (Wharton), and doesn't mince words. "I'm a cynic by nature, Tom. But I'm ready to be proven wrong. We've invested in Breakout and done a lot of kaizen events. Frankly speaking, we haven't seen any ROI."*

"There's a lot more to Lean than kaizen events, Arnold."

"We have a bottom line problem, and a top line problem. Our biggest problem is cost. We have a fundamental imbalance between revenue and expense."

"Healthcare is not unique," Andy says. "Today, cost is everybody's problem. Lower cost and better quality. It's hard, but it can be done without firing team members."

"Can you help me with that?" Penniman asks. "At Grandview, cost walks on two legs. Sorry, but it's true. How are we going to reduce cost without firing people?"

* Return on Investment.

"What's your annual attrition rate?" Andy asks.

"About 10 percent overall, higher for nurses."

"What if we reduce workforce by 2 percent each year through attrition, Arnold-san, while providing better service? How about spending on drugs, materials, and equipment? Do you have waste there? What about the cost of readmits, infections, and medical errors?"

Penniman is taking it all in. "What about the top line? ACA* is shrinking our revenue, and increasing our safety net patient load."

"I've seen a ton of delay waste in the Cancer Center," I tell him. "I understand it's the same across Grandview's major service lines. What if we could increase throughput and reduce length of stay by, say, 10 percent per year, in your high value care lines?

"That would be big," Penniman says. "But I'm stuck on the *how.*"

"Mr. Saito and I will teach you how. If you all do your homework, you'll get at least 10-percent improvement per year on all your main indicators. *If you do your homework…*"

"That's fair," Penniman says.

"May we ask a favor?" Andy says. "Can you take Tom-san and me through Grandview financials? We need your insight and understanding."

"Happy to do that."

Kayla O'Leary is the chief strategy officer, a Columbia MBA with strawberry blonde hair, freckles, and big green glasses. "Please call me Pinky. I'm really interested in Hoshin Kanri. I understand it's a Toyota Best Practice."

Pinky is the architect of Grandview's Five-Year Strategy, which comprises more than 250 "focused initiatives" and

---

* Patient Protection and Affordable Care Act (aka Obamacare).

hundreds of "critical indicators." Where did these come from? Largely from "Big Friday"—a monthly meeting during which senior managers propose project ideas. If a majority of people give the thumbs up, your initiative is accepted and goes into the hopper. Evidently, nothing gets the thumbs down.

There was a second, somewhat sinister, source of top-down initiatives, which Pinky called "central policy," meaning HNYC and the state.

If you don't understand the problem, you buffer with volume. That's another Andy Saito principle. In other words, you start pressing buttons frantically, hoping something will happen. Something does happen—the improvement pipeline turns to cement. Seems people at senior levels are pressing buttons all over the place.

"We will teach you Hoshin Kanri," Andy says.

"We call it Strategy *Deployment*," I add. "How do we translate critical strategic gaps into activity? How do we screen activities so we don't overload our improvement pipeline? How do we involve everybody in improvement work?"

Pinky's face is blank. It's not her fault. She's been taught that Strategy comprises senior leaders developing clever plans and everybody else doing as they're told. I imagine Madeleine and Arnold think the same way. The last box in their flow chart is *Implement*, which I call "and now miracles will happen."

"Please take us through your analysis, Pinky-san," says Andy. "Help us to understand the strategic problems." We agree to meet again next week.

Fox, Harper, McKnight, Kwan, Penniman, and O'Leary (Figure 6.2) are Grandview's most senior leaders and the ones we'll work with most closely. We spend another hour meeting the vice presidents of the various medical specialties and corporate functions.

FIGURE 6.2
The usual suspects. Copyright 2015 Lean Pathways Inc.

Gwen escorts Andy and me to our new office, next to Carol Kwan's, for a scheduled call with Rachel Armstrong. Gwen introduces us to Kim Banks, our executive assistant. We exchange pleasantries. Kim offers to serve coffee or tea and we accept.

It's a nice enough office with a fine view of the East River and the Williamsburg Bridge to the south. I think of the bridge's famous sign, *Leaving Brooklyn, oy vey!*

Gwen takes a sip of tea. "Well, gentlemen, what do you think?"

"Many generals," says Andy.

"And tension among the most senior," I add.

"Dr. Fox is a lovely man," Gwen says, "but he's tired. The staff adore him but feel betrayed because he hasn't protected their jobs. Bob will support you internally, but has limited influence.

He'll be a great advocate in the mayor's office though, and will buy us time if we need it.

"Madeleine Harper and Arnold Penniman will be our biggest challenges," Gwen continues. "Dr. Harper isn't happy with your appointment. She's very smart and ambitious. Her husband runs a big hedge fund and is a major donor. She also has connections in the mayor's office. We have to be careful.

"Arnold came to us from Goldman Sachs. Like Madeleine, he's rich and well connected. He's a straight numbers guy. Give him evidence that the Toyota system works and he'll be a big supporter. Beneath Arnold's CFO veneer, I detect a human heart. He could have stayed at Goldman Sachs. Arnold's just doing what he knows, which is cost-cutting. Nurses and other front line staff have been decimated."

"Very strange," Andy says. "The hospital is firing front line staff."

Gwen nods. "Dr. Harper's attitude hasn't helped. In a recent Town Hall meeting she tried to justify the latest firings by saying Grandview has to provide 'exceptional value,' and can't afford to 'carry people in twelve-dollar-an-hour jobs.' Then she offered her eight-million-dollar loft in SoHo as an example of 'exceptional value.' She said Grandview staff needs to emulate her architect and engineer. Can you imagine?"

"Oy vey."

"Dr. Harper was on the short list for my job," says Gwen. "Grandview's problems were a big black mark for her."

We absorb this. "Might work our way," I offer. "We need Madeleine to succeed, and she needs us to remove the black mark."

"There's tension between Carol and Madeleine," Gwen continues. "Carol grew up in Chinatown, in a small laundry and tailoring shop. She is fiercely loyal to her nurses and has fought every downsizing. Madeleine would like to fire her.

"Dr. McKnight is a fine physician and a good man. He doesn't want to be CMO but is taking one for the team. He was much happier as head of the ED. He believes in transparency and letting people know when we mess up. He's had major run-ins with Legal.

"Pinky is bright but doesn't understand the front line at all. They call her 'Madame PowerPoint.' Her parents are New York gentry and major donors. Big Friday is a disaster—each month more ill-conceived projects get dumped into the hopper. Very little gets finished."

"It was strange to see Dr. Brewster," says Andy.

Gwen exhales. "He generates a lot of publicity, but I've heard he's not the world's greatest surgeon."

"How do we know if a surgery is good or bad?" Andy asks.

"Great question," Gwen says. "Please challenge our surgeons with it."

Kim comes in with tea and coffee and sets up the polycom for our teleconference. Rachel's voice rolls out of the speakers. "Aloha from Taylor City, Michigan! How are you all?"

"Good day so far," I say. "The next several weeks Andy and I will walk the main hospital service lines and support groups, and review current management systems, activities, and results. We'll pull in the senior team and have a draft strategy in four weeks. We should be aligned and ready for deployment in January.

"Sounds good," Rachel says. "Gwen, what do you think?"

"I'm okay with the timeline, with one proviso," says Gwen. "We need some quick wins. A lot of people are watching. We have to show them something."

"We can get quick wins in the Cancer Center," I tell them.

"Very good," Gwen says. "Please choose activities that are scalable. We have seventeen hospitals and dozens of clinics."

"Shared lateral learning is most important," says Andy. "We call it Yokoten."

We agree on an overall timeline, and on a regular weekly teleconference. Kim summarizes her meeting notes for us. Rachel signs off. Gwen then gives us each a hug, and hurries to a waiting cab.

I walk to the window. The East River is a gray rag, mirroring the sky. The Williamsburg Bridge is gray too, and jammed with cars leaving Brooklyn.

"Well, sensei, what do you think?"

"We have good support. But we will need quick wins to sustain it."

"How about the Grandview leadership team?"

"Senior leaders are all capable and well-educated. But their thinking way is maybe not so good."

*Genchi genbutsu** time. I ask Kim to set up a regular walk schedule with Bill McKnight and Carol Kwan. Dr. McKnight replies by text. We'll start tomorrow morning in the ED.

* *

"Well what do you think of our new senseis?" Madeleine Harper asked.

"They seem like decent chaps," said Dr. Fox. "I've no doubt they have great knowledge. But do they know healthcare? Will they be accepted by our staff?"

"I remain a skeptic," Madeleine said. "Human beings are not automobiles. I'm sure Tom and Andy are capable, but have they ever cared for the sick? Have they studied the healing arts?"

Arnold Penniman was trying not to show his annoyance. Look at these two, he thought. Grandview is a train wreck and they're nit-picking. Through discipline and force of will,

* Go see the real place (*gemba*).

Arnold had pulled himself out of Philadelphia's mean streets and into Wharton and Goldman Sachs. His wife, Marie, persuaded him to take the Grandview CFO position. "We've got to give something back, sugar."

Arnold was a process and a numbers guy and sensed Tom and Andy were exactly what Grandview needed. He looked at Madeleine and John some more.

"I got a good overall feeling," Arnold said. "I think Tom and Andy are the real deal. I need to see some quick results though."

Study Questions

1. Arnold Penniman suggests that in healthcare, "Cost walks on two legs."
   a. Do you agree or disagree? Explain your answer.
   b. If an organization is in financial difficulty, as Grandview Hospital is, shouldn't they be able to downsize the workforce? Explain your answer.
   c. What are the risks in doing so?
   d. Describe any personal experience you've had. Can you suggest any learning points or reflections?
2. Grandview has both "top line" (revenue) and "bottom line" (profit/loss) problems.
   a. How can Lean methods improve the top line?
   b. Describe any corresponding personal experience you've had. Can you suggest any reflections or learning points?
   c. How can Lean methods improve the bottom line?
   d. Describe any personal experience you've had. Any reflections or learning points?
3. Dr. Harper, COO, believes in "empowering" the front line. "It's your show," she tells the nurses. Carol Kwan, CNO, calls it abandonment.

   a. Can you outline the two points of view?
   b. Describe any corresponding personal experiences. Can you suggest any learning points or reflections?
4. "Strategy is something senior leaders do. The rest of the organization does what it's told."
   a. Do you agree or disagree with this approach to strategy? Explain your answer.
   b. What are the strengths and weaknesses of this approach? Can you describe an example from your personal experience?
5. What does "deployment" mean? Sketch out your answer using as few written words as possible. Don't worry if you "can't draw." Stick figures, arrows, and circles are fine.

7

What's Happening behind the Curtain?

Hospitals are a shadowy realm behind a dark curtain where strange things happen (Figure 7.1). Specialists appear and ask questions. Technicians arrive and take your loved one away for tests. Appointments are made, for more tests, more specialists. Then the darkest realm of all—surgery.

If you're lucky things work out. If not…

I want to draw back the curtain and flood the dark realm with light. I want patients and their families to know, at a glance, if things are okay or not okay, what's going to happen next, and why. I want hospital errors to be visible, and the mess to be obvious.

I know the dark curtain has always been there, woven of isolation, complexity, and self-interest. And I understand miracles happen there too. Polio, diphtheria, malaria, smallpox, tetanus, and other deadly diseases have for now either been eradicated or nearly so. Acute lymphocytic leukemia is no longer a death sentence for children. Harry's right—it's a great paradox. Miracles happened within the deep hospital silos, and all too often, terrible and entirely avoidable tragedy across them.

FIGURE 7.1
The dark realm. Copyright 2015 Lean Pathways Inc.

Our first Grandview walk is with Dr. McKnight in the Emergency Department (ED). On the way we pay a visit to Grandview's internal kaizen (aka Breakout) team. Our Taylor Motors colleagues, who will coach and support them, had arrived the day before.

Antonio Villarreal, who will act as senior sensei, is a hip and creative Mexican who designs theatre sets in his spare time.

His stamping plant is world class. Antonio gives me a bear hug. "Como estan amigos. Long time, no see."

Becky Johnson is a mechanical engineer from Fort Worth, a devout Christian who has just returned from aid projects in East Africa. Becky helped transform NJMM's chaotic Weld shop into an oasis of order and stability.

Benny Walton is a sales and marketing star who grew up in Detroit and survived its scary public school system. Benny was a college chess champion and still plays high-level tournaments through the Internet. "Chess taught me how to focus," he once told me.

Elaine Miyazaki is a business process specialist and a black belt in Shotokan karate. She's a third-generation Japanese-American, and has a working knowledge of Japanese and Mandarin. "Konbanwa, Elaine-san," I say, in my sensei voice, part of our martial arts shtick. She replies with comic gruffness. "*Arigato gozeimas*, Tom-san!"

Antonio introduces us to the Breakout team. Danny Kaufman is the director, a Brooklyn-born industrial engineer who cut his teeth at a major automotive parts company. Danny is evidently devoted to his wife and new baby, whose photos are all over his cubicle. "Our family was in the garment trade—leather gloves," he tells me. "Garment district, the whole bit. Low-cost offshore production put us out of business."

"How did you end up at Grandview, Danny?"

"I spent ten years in automotive engineering. We were happy living in Michigan. Grandview head-hunted me. There's no place like home. Been here three years now. It's definitely not manufacturing."

Danny's team is composed of seven young people with a range of backgrounds including nursing, physiotherapy, IT, and manufacturing. They seemed smart and well-trained, though unsure of themselves. I asked Danny to take us through the Breakout team's purpose, strategy, and current condition. We walk over to the huddle board.

The Breakout team's purpose is unclear and the link to Grandview's overall purpose, tenuous. To be fair, the latter hasn't been clearly communicated. The strategy appears to entail continuous kaizen events. Problem statements are often vague and root causes murky. Some kaizens have resulted in focused countermeasures. Most are essentially scavenger hunts for waste. Little has stuck.

The team's understanding of individual parts of the Toyota system seems to be okay. But they haven't yet grasped how the parts fit together or the underlying thinking. There also seems to be a gap in practical experience. I can't see them handling a difficult surgeon or snarly charge nurse.

"We've worked for months in the ED and Surgical Services," says Danny. "Front line team members get excited and do good work. Management pays lip service, then disappears. Physicians undermine our work if it means any change to their routines.

"Following standards is optional around here, even basic safety and hygiene standards. Nobody checks, and nobody calls them on it. The stuff we see would be unthinkable in manufacturing."

The words hang there, a flag of defeat.

"That's all going to change," I tell them.

* *

Andy and I walk over to the ED to meet Dr. McKnight. In the ensuing weeks, we'll walk all the major care lines and visit all the main support groups. The former comprise Medicine, Psychiatry, Surgery, Emergency and Trauma, Pediatrics, Women and Newborn, Oncology, Cardiovascular, Bariatrics, and Orthopedics. We learned that "care line" means a handful of reasonably well-defined service categories.

Grandview support groups included Pharmacy, Imaging, Laboratories (including Microbiology, Pathology, Hematology, Genetics, and Autopsy Services), Blood Bank, Housekeeping, Nutrition, Information Services, Social Work, and Medical Instrument Reprocessing (meaning decontamination of soiled materials and equipment).

* *

Our first few days are tough. Nothing can prepare you for an NYC ED. We see a young woman expire from a knife wound to her stomach. Multiple "ped" cases—pedestrians or bicyclists who've been hit by cars. A man with a butcher knife in his chest, still alive and miraculously "stable." A bariatric patient who'd fallen and suffered multiple fractures, and a carpenter with missing fingers. Stroke and heart attack victims, terrified family members around them. Psychiatric patients, poor souls with ravaged minds, some through life experience or substance abuse, others through some tragedy of brain chemistry. "It's like a thunderstorm in my brain," one haggard young woman said to the nurse.

We also see obnoxious "patients" making absurd demands. "I want a room and a nice hot lunch," a woman said to the triage nurse. "What are your symptoms?" "Well, I just feel weak." "Sorry, you're going to have to wait." A flood of profanity followed.

"Is there any way to dissuade such people?" I ask Dr. McKnight.

"Security will remove them if they get hostile or if they interfere with somebody's care," he replies. "It's part of a broader problem. How do we discourage non-emergency cases from flooding the ED?"

Mornings in the ED leave Andy and me full of admiration. Our colleagues are gallant knights surging into the breach, risking infectious disease, physical assault, and burnout. In heart-rending circumstances, they remain gracious and good-natured. "To be helpful, you have to separate yourself to an extent," says Dr. McKnight.

Yet there are obvious problems. There's little visual management, (other than admonitions—DON'T DO THAT!). There are no ED team boards or daily huddles. Shift handovers seem haphazard. What happened yesterday or last week? Are there any important trends, hot spots, or learning points? Nobody seems to know. Nor is there any discernible improvement work.

During down periods Andy and I chat with the ED nurses. We learn that a typical day comprises dozens of different tasks. The most common include reading and assessing vital signs, taking blood (venipuncture), hanging intravenous (IV) lines, and administering drugs and treatments.

For many of these tasks, most nurses can articulate the content and sequence of the work and highlight key points. But when we ask about process standards, we get funny looks. "Our standard operating procedures are useless," a charge nurse tells us.

"How do you train new team members?" Andy asks.

"We learn on the job."

We watch nurses cycle through IV bag preparation, one of the most basic tasks. They're frequently interrupted—five times for one charge nurse.

"Why were you interrupted so many times?" I ask him.

He shakes his head. "Complete nonsense. I got two texts about a medication change I already knew about. Don't they know I read my shift reports? Dr. Saunders, who was walking by, felt she just *had* to tell me one more time. The other interruptions were my nurses looking for stuff, a bariatric bed and some syringes."

"I counted ten or twelve steps in the IV process," I tell him. "With all those interruptions, how can you remember what step you're on?"

"It's easy to forget," he admits, "but if you do, they'll blame you!"

Then he gets another text and hurries away.

"People do not trust existing processes," says Andy.

The next morning, Bill McKnight draws back the curtain for us. The EMS team brought in a stroke victim, a terrified immigrant who could have been my mother. We watch the Stroke Team in action, while Dr. McKnight explains what's happening. A stroke, we learn, means that blood supply to the brain is interrupted. Brain cells begin to die at once, so speed is everything. A stroke could be *ischemic*, meaning an artery is blocked, or *hemorrhagic*, meaning an artery has burst. There are clear emergency protocols for each, but the Stroke Team needs a CT scan to make the call.

The ED doctor whispers in the poor woman's ear as the respiratory therapist is called to insert the IV needle containing contrasting fluid into her bloodstream before the CT scan. The patient waits for the stroke-specific CT scanner to be cleared of non-emergency cases. This takes about twenty minutes.

"No fast track?" Andy asks.

"There should be," says Dr. McKnight.

It turns out to be an ischemic stroke—an artery is blocked. The neurologist writes an order for a clot-busting drug, tPA (tissue plasminogen activator), and faxes it to Pharmacy, which will take twenty minutes to fast-track the order. Meanwhile, the patient is wheeled to a room with us in tow. I feel like an intruder, but how else can you understand what's happening? To his credit, Dr. McKnight wants us to understand.

An X-ray technologist appears and is about to wheel the patient out for chest X-rays. Dr. McKnight intervenes and explains that the patient is awaiting critical drugs. A few minutes later the tPA arrives and is administered. Within an hour the patient is able to move her arms again and is expected to recover fully.

We're silent on the way back to the ED. The Imaging department's CT fast-track process has failed. Andy chatted with the pharmacy technician. Apparently, Pharmacy's fast-track also fails from time to time. And but for Dr. McKnight, the X-ray tech would have taken the patient away at the worst possible time.

Dr. McKnight is embarrassed. "Sorry about this."

"The problem is in the process, Bill," I say. "Nothing wrong with your people."

"You're kind to say so, Tom. We need help, as you can see. I'm afraid I have to go now. See you tomorrow morning."

Dr. McKnight has shone a light into the dark realm. His decency outweighed his embarrassment.

Andy and I walk over to the ED's suppliers—Imaging and Pharmacy. We ask basic questions. Who are your customers? What do they need? What are your top three problems? How are you doing right now?

Blank stares. Nobody can clearly articulate the needs of their customer, the ED, with respect to turnaround time, quality, or volume. Or how many fast-track request failures there have been last week or last month. It's in the computer, somebody said. A dark realm within a dark realm, I thought.

Neither Imaging nor Pharmacy has a team board with customer metrics, or daily huddles to discuss hot spots, or any evidence of improvement work.

Connections between the ED and downstream receiving departments also seem dodgy. Referring to a colleague downstream, an ED doctor said, "Why does she keep asking the same questions?" The same applied to upstream groups such as the ambulance service. Evidently, ambulances from other hospitals routinely arrived unannounced, adding to the chaos.

It takes several weeks for Andy and me to fully grasp what we were seeing. We begin to realize that the ED is a microcosm of the entire hospital. Similar problems exist in all the care lines and support departments we visit. The ED's intensity just brings them out quicker.

I'm troubled by a chat I had with Doreen Howard, an experienced and well-respected ED director. Normally Doreen was cheerful but this late afternoon she looked broken. "Are you okay?" I asked.

"No I'm not okay," she said. "I'm going to level with you. This place is killing me. Every day there's a new demand, a new initiative, another bureaucratic brainwave. More meetings, more project charters, more silly metrics. And they also say, 'Oh, we'll need two resources too.' *I don't have any resources to spare!* And they still want me to run my ED and 'continuously improve.' No offense, I really like the Breakout team, but where the hell am I going to get the time for kaizen? You seem like a good guy. You say you want to understand what's really happening. Well, there you go."

And one last thing. I'm tired of fighting Dr. Brewster. Know what we call him? *Dr. Hodad*—hands of death and destruction. He makes his own rules but nobody wants to confront him."

I shudder. Did a Dr. Hodad operate on Uncle Angie? "Thanks for your honesty and courage, Doreen. This is all going to change, I promise you."

Grandview is rife with every kind of waste, especially delay, errors, and over-processing. They're also awash in variation—in patient volume, rate of arrival, and length of stay, and in the four Ms—Manpower, Methods, Materials, and Machinery. Continuous chaos has fueled a corrosive fatalism. "Nothing we can do" is a common refrain. Good people drowning in a sea of broken processes.

Kind of like New Jersey Motor Manufacturing a decade ago.

* *

Harry and Tom settle into a booth. The Humpty Dumpty's Saturday afternoon rush is subsiding. "How are you finding Grandview?" Harry asks.

"I'm shocked," says Tom. "My local dry cleaner has better processes. Basic things like referral, registration, and scheduling are a mess. I've never seen anything like it."

"Now you know why chemotherapy bags are being mislabeled."

"Any progress on that one?" Tom asks.

"They appointed a 'senior level task force'," Harry says, "which is code for 'nothing is going to happen.' "

Tom shakes his head. "What've I gotten myself into, Harry?"

Study Questions

1. Tom, still hurting from Uncle Angie's death, describes healthcare as a "shadowy realm behind a dark curtain."
   a. Do you agree with this characterization? Explain your answer.
   b. Tom suggests the curtain is woven of "isolation, complexity and self-interest."
      i. Do you agree or disagree? Explain your answer.
      ii. Are there any other important factors?
2. Tom and Andy observe multiple failures in a Code Stroke.
   a. Are these failures plausible? Explain your answer.
   b. What are possible root causes for each failure?
   c. What are possible countermeasures?
3. Tom suggests that the problem is almost always in the process, not the people.
   a. Do you agree or disagree? Explain your answer.
   b. Can you provide at least three examples that support Tom's suggestion?
   c. Can you provide any examples that do not support Tom's suggestion?
   d. Can you suggest any reflections or learning points?

8

Developing Our Strategy

Strategy is storytelling, narrative. Our ancestors on the African savannah fifty thousand years ago told stories at day's end. They didn't show PowerPoint.

You have to answer simple questions in a compelling way (Figure 8.1):

1. Who are we?
2. Where are we going?
3. How do we get there?

Thanks to Andy, Strategy Deployment (aka *Hoshin Kanri*) has been our compass and spear point at Taylor Motors. There are four "simple" steps*:

1. Develop the plan.
2. Deploy the plan.
3. Monitor the plan.
4. Improve the system.

* For a detailed description of Strategy Deployment, the interested reader is referred to *Getting the Right Things Done: A Leader's Guide to Planning and Execution* (Cambridge, MA: Lean Enterprise Institute, 2006) by Pascal Dennis.

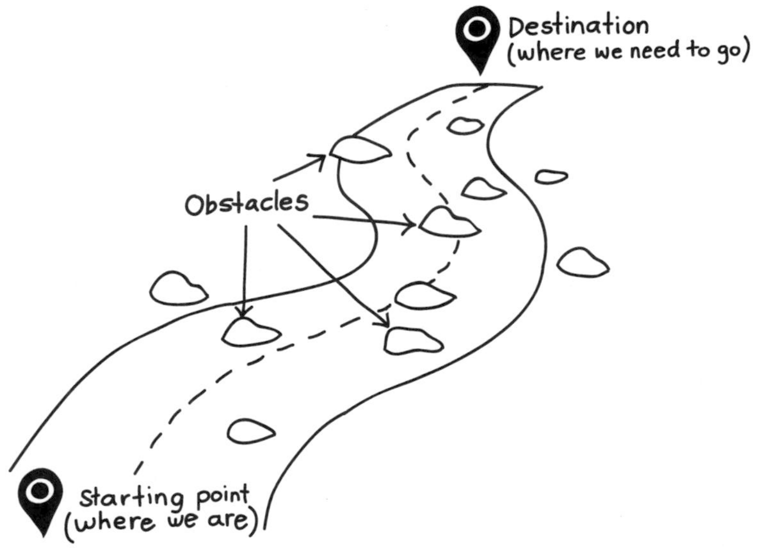

FIGURE 8.1
The road image. Copyright 2015 Lean Pathways Inc.

We begin by defining Purpose (True North)—something for the head, something for the heart (Figure 8.2). The head goal comprises hard targets, the business results we must achieve. The heart goal (*hoshin*) is an expression of values, direction, and commitment.

Then we figure out what's preventing us and write our "strategy A3s"—one-page storyboards on 11" × 17" paper (Figure 8.3). The left-hand side is "Pain," the right hand, "Hope." The A3 story goes something like this: "Here's where the shoe pinches. Here's why, and our proposed remedy."

A sound A3 entails a hypothesis. "If we do *this*, we believe *that* will happen." We run the experiment, observe what happens and adjust as required. It's strategic *management*—strategy as

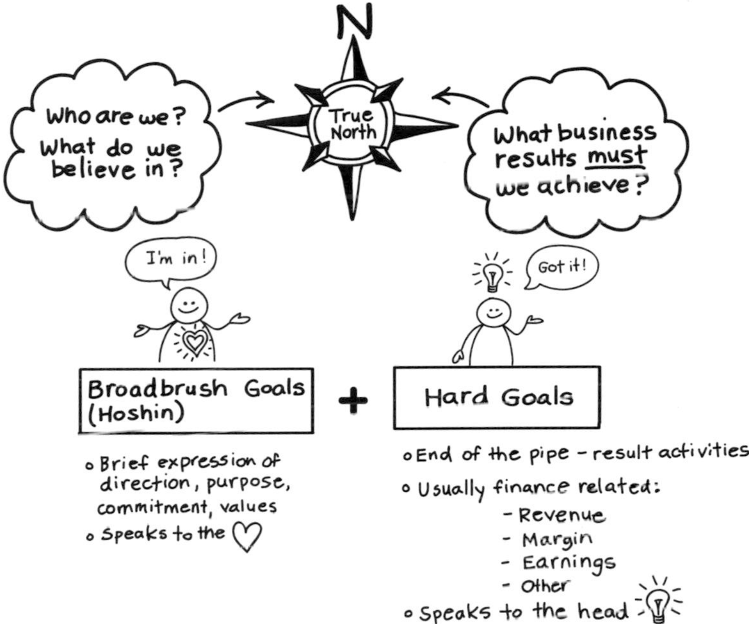

FIGURE 8.2
True North. Copyright 2015 Lean Pathways Inc.

an iterative, interactive process, instead of the tired "one-and-done" approach.[*,†]

The Strategy Development process is a fractal and thus applies at multiple levels (Figure 8.4).[‡] We can zoom out to the entire enterprise or zoom in to the front line unit. It comprises the following steps:

Step 1. Define the gap.
Step 2. Ask "what's preventing us?" Brainstorming uses analytical tools. Go see and validate possible causes.

---

* Ibid.

† See also Chapter 5 of Pascal Dennis, *The Remedy: Bringing Lean Out of the Factory to Transform the Entire Organization* (Hoboken, NJ: John Wiley & Sons, 2010).

‡ Pascal Dennis, *Getting the Right Things Done*, p. 96.

A3 Theme

What is our objective?

Target

Target

Action Plan

What, When, Who....

①

②

③

What happened last year?

Activity	Test	Result	Meaning?

What's our analysis and rationale for this year's activities?

What might go wrong? What are we unsure of? Contingency Plans:

Signatures: ____ ____ ____

Author: ________

Date: ______ Version: ______

Strategy – A3 Storyboard

FIGURE 8.3
Telling stories with A3s. Copyright 2015 Lean Pathways Inc.

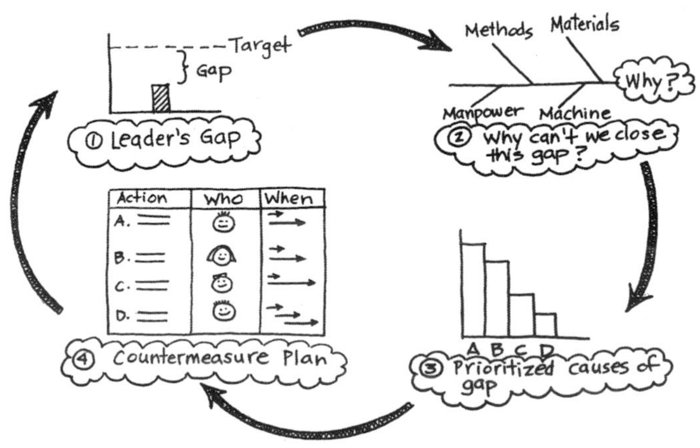

FIGURE 8.4
Strategy Development process. Copyright 2015 Lean Pathways Inc.

Step 3. Prioritize possible causes.
Step 4. Develop your hypothesis and action plan.

Most common failure modes:

- Not defining the gap
- Jumping from step 1 to 4
- Superficial causal analysis
- Not prioritizing causes, or prioritizing without data
- Actions don't address the most important causes

Step 2, Deploy the Plan, means breaking the obstacles into bite-sized chunks and engaging the requisite teams in removing them (Figure 8.5).* Our ideal is total involvement.

Deployment has been the key in our factories. Selection is less important. You can survive a marginal plan, but not a poor deployment (Figure 8.6).

Senior management's job, therefore, is to

1. Define purpose clearly
2. Identify the biggest obstacles
3. Create an atmosphere conducive to initiative and creativity
4. Reduce hassle

I love Andy's river metaphor (Figure 8.7). Senior leaders define Purpose (the sea) and the banks of the river (our strategic "design space," if you will). They let the water find its way and don't worry if it sloshes a bit left or right. They check in regularly and remove obstacles.

---

* Dave Meier and Jeff Liker, *The Toyota Way Field Book* (New York: McGraw-Hill Education, 2005).

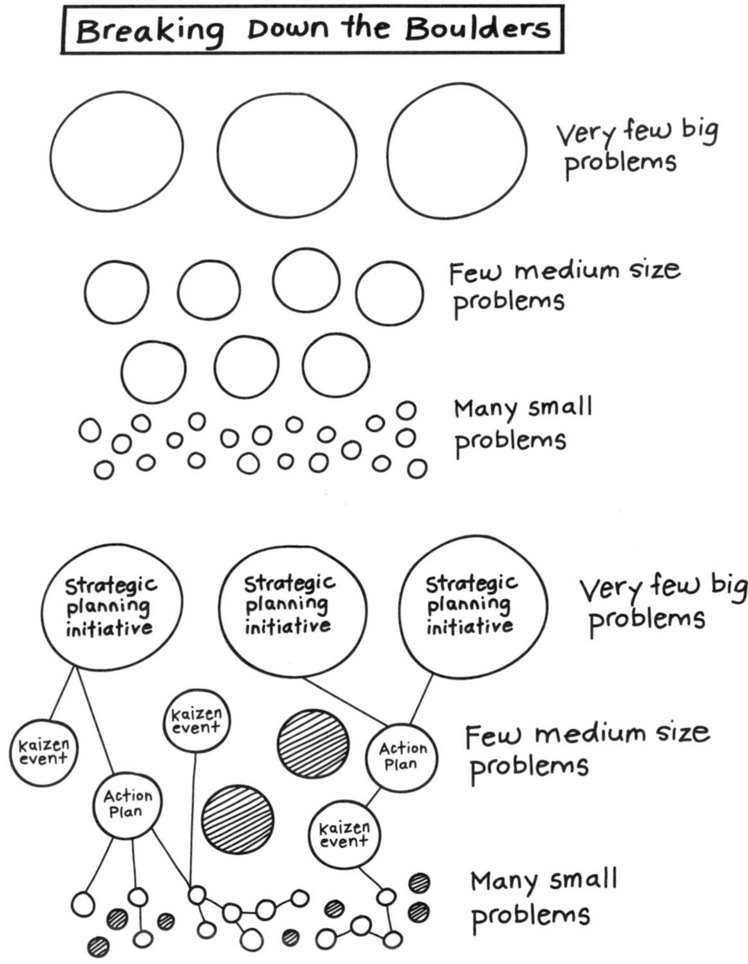

FIGURE 8.5
Connected problem solving. Copyright 2015 Lean Pathways Inc.

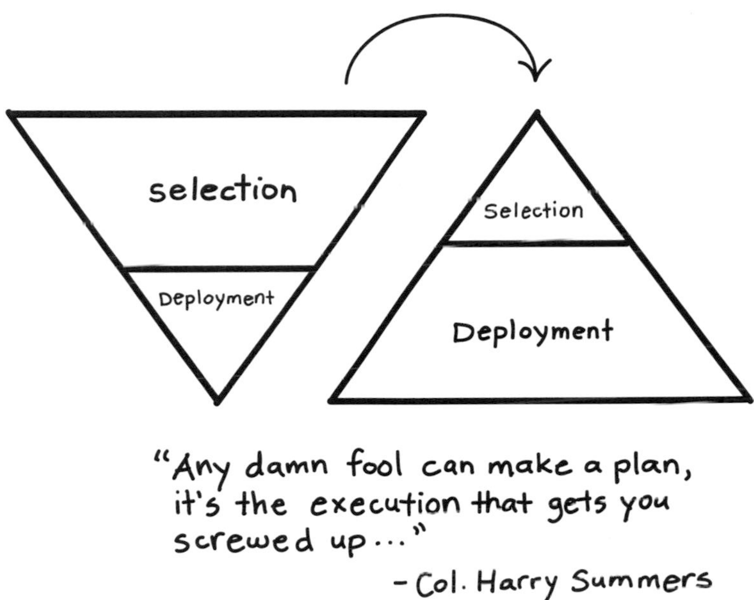

FIGURE 8.6
Selection versus Deployment. Copyright 2015 Lean Pathways Inc.

But many of us have been taught the opposite. Many leaders believe improvement entails "very smart people, just like us" defining the perfect strategy, and everyone else doing what they're told. That's what I learned in engineering and business school.

And nobody talks about it. Our core mental model around leadership is invisible. Could John, Madeleine, Arnold, and the rest learn to lead in this way?

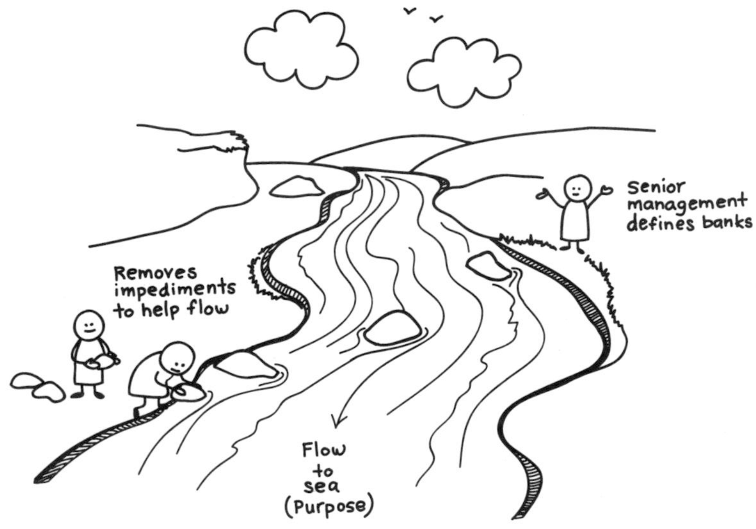

FIGURE 8.7
The river metaphor. Copyright 2015 Lean Pathways Inc.

Grandview's stated purpose is "to provide high quality health-care to all, regardless of their ability to pay." It was a good *hoshin*—Andy called it a "Noble Goal." Now we need hard targets.

Andy and I take senior leaders through the Strategy Deployment process. After intense debate we agree on four focus areas and the following True North metrics (Figure 8.8)*:

- Patient Safety and Quality
  - Preventable mortality
  - Infection rate
  - Medication errors
- Service Delivery
  - Throughput
  - Length of stay
  - Access

* With a tip of the hat to Dr. John Toussaint, Dr. Dean Gruner, and the Thedacare team.

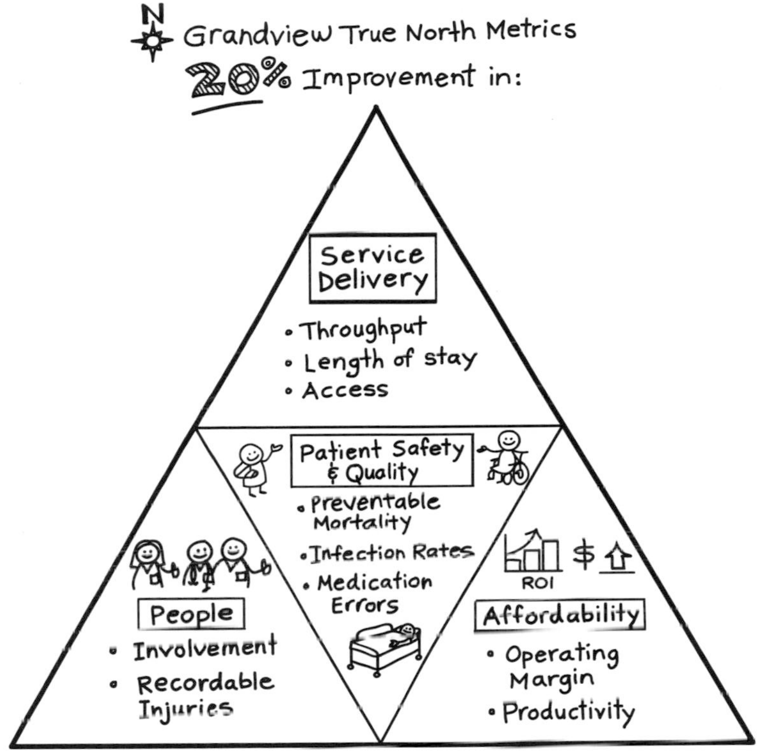

FIGURE 8.8
Grandview True North metrics. Copyright 2015 Lean Pathways Inc.

- People
  - Team member involvement (metric tbd)
  - Recordable injuries
- Affordability
  - Operating margin
  - Productivity

Our hard targets will be a 20-percent improvement for each by fiscal year-end, which we feel will satisfy Gwen Carter and the mayor's office. To communicate True North we come up with the following image. With time, our "True North triangle" will become ubiquitous.

Each focus area will have a "mother A3" strategy written by a senior leader. We'll deploy these in our pilot areas to start. Pilot areas will translate mother A3 strategies into focused front line activity ("baby A3s") (Figure 8.9). Our goal: one improvement activity per focus area, per pilot zone unit by year-end.

A critical early step is cleaning up the "Project Pipeline," currently clogged with more than 250 top-down "initiatives"

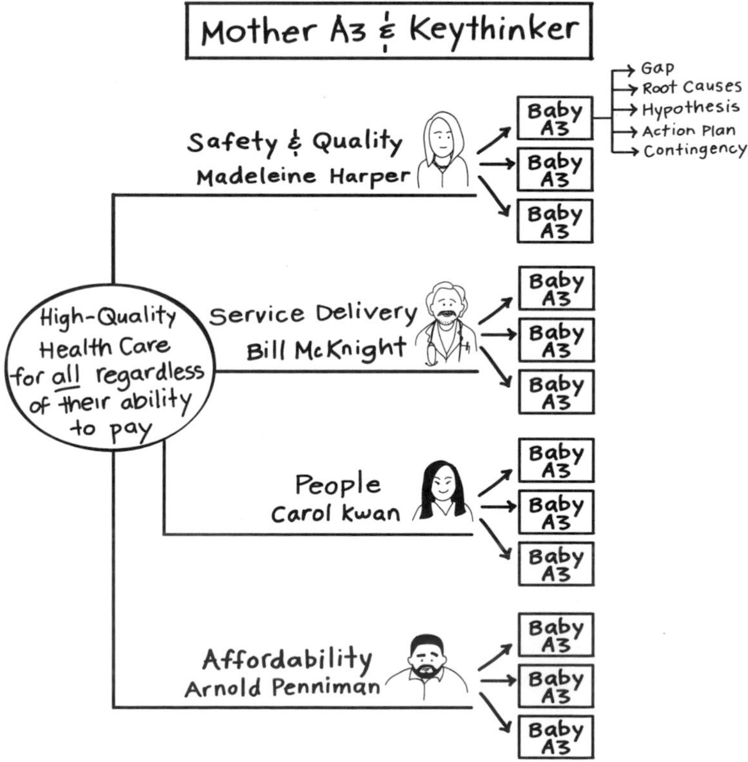

FIGURE 8.9
Grandview Strategy Deployment tree. Copyright 2015 Lean Pathways Inc.

chasing more than 300 "targets." Big Friday provides no meaningful screen. A leader's upward mobility, and often, their compensation, depends on their hobbyhorse's acceptance. So everybody says "Yes," knowing they'll get the same when their pet project is up. No wonder Doreen is burning out.

But there's a bigger underlying problem, which Harry says is endemic to the industry. Many top-down projects are foisted on Grandview by HNYC- and state-level bureaucrats far from the *gemba** and absent of any real understanding of the front line.

Remote policy touts are feathering their nests at our expense. Their "central policy" initiatives mean endless charters and meetings, confusing metrics, tiresome report outs, and the like. They consume scarce capacity we needed to support our, *Grandview*'s, strategy.

The result is a Bermuda Triangle of management (Figure 8.10).† It devours energy, morale, and hope, and shatters focus and alignment. Without protection, we'll be sucked down like everybody else. We'll take it up with Gwen Carter.

Andy and I introduce Production Physics, and in particular, Little's Law and the Law of Utilization. Nobody has ever heard of them.

LITTLE'S LAW

The fundamental equation of production physics. Little's Law applies anywhere there is a queue of work.

Little's Law:

Cycle Time = Work in Process (WIP) ÷ Throughput, or

Throughput = Work in Process (WIP) ÷ Cycle Time

---

* The real place, usually the front line, where value is created.

† Dr. Dan Jones' phrase.

FIGURE 8.10
The Bermuda Triangle of management. Copyright 2015 Lean Pathways Inc.

Definitions:

- *Throughput* is the average output of a service or production process (e.g., number of patients, laboratory tests, or projects completed) per unit time (e.g., patients per day, tests per week, or projects per year).
- *Cycle time* for a given care line or work flow is the average time from the arrival of the patient, test, or project to arrival at the end of line.
- *Work in process* is the inventory accumulated between the start and end points of a care line or work flow (e.g., the number of patients between admitting and release, or the number of projects in the queue).

Implications:

- For a fixed capacity process, *cycle time and WIP are proportional*. Thus, if we release twice as much work into our system then cycle time *doubles*. Moreover, high WIP levels also mean high operating expenses.
- To increase throughput, we can flood the workplace with patients, tests, or projects (the mass production or batch and queue approach); or we can reduce inventory and reduce cycle time by reducing waste (Toyota's approach).

Related laws:

- The Law of Variability: Increasing variability inevitably degrades the performance of the system.

- The Law of Variability Buffering: Variability in a system will be buffered by some combination of inventory, capacity, and time.

Walter Hopp and Mark Spearman
Factory Physics (New York: McGraw-Hill, 2000)

THE LAW OF UTILIZATION

If a resource in a flow increases utilization without making other changes, work in process and cycle times will increase in a highly nonlinear manner. When utilization exceeds 80 percent work in process and cycle times explode.

Walter Hopp and Mark Spearman
Factory Physics (New York: McGraw-Hill, 2000)

"Less is more," I tell the senior team. "By overfilling the pipeline, we drive utilization above 80 percent. Cycle times explode and the pipeline turns to cement. Big implications for patient flow too, as we'll see."

Production Physics strikes a chord. "No wonder we never finish anything," says Arnold Penniman.

"You'd think we'd know how to triage," says Dr. McKnight.

"But many of our projects come from HNYC and the state," Pinky says.

"I know, Pinky," I say. "Andy and I will talk to Gwen Carter. In the interim, let's manage what's in our control."

"What is the countermeasure to too many projects?" Andy asks.

Several voices ring out. "Improve the project selection process." In the ensuing brainstorming session we define the following project selection criteria:

1. Clearly related to True North and at least one critical True North metric?
2. Problem and impact clearly defined?
3. Root causes identified?
4. Hypothesis articulated? Countermeasures clear?
5. Action plan defined with clear milestones and expected outcomes?
6. Pilot plan developed, where appropriate?
7. Proposal summarized on one clear, understandable page?
8. Clear check process?

Pinky's project management team will put existing projects through the screen. Those that meet the standard will be put before a subcommittee that will classify them as A, B, or C. A's will go into the pipeline—if there's an opening. B's go into a parking lot, and C's are rejected (Figure 8.11).

We'll keep an upper limit on top-down project using the "Close one—Start one" approach. To pull a new project into the pipeline, we have to close one first.

We're freeing up time and energy. Now we have to get front line activity going. It's almost nonexistent at Grandview. Top-down improvement tends to be orderly and dumb. Bottom-up improvement is chaotic but smart (Figure 8.12).*

Eighty percent of your improvement effort should be at the front line, Andy says. As a rule, the stronger the organization,

* Carlson's Law. "Carlson's Law—An interview with SRI International President & CEO Dr. Curtis Carlson." *San Francisco Chronicle*, August 29, 2011. Retrieved November 22, 2011.

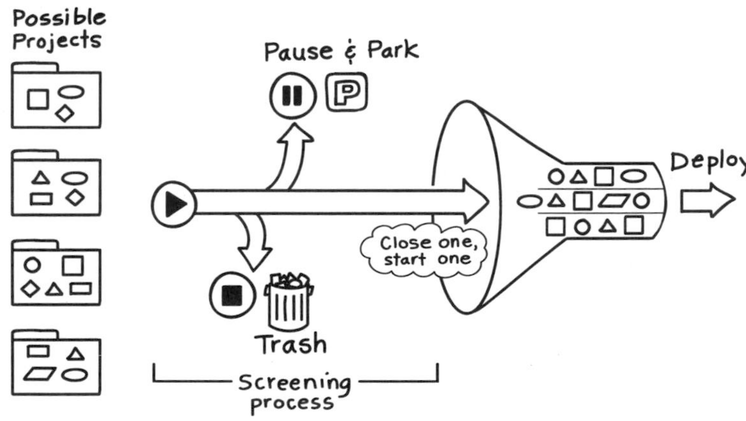

FIGURE 8.11
Slimming down the project pipeline. Copyright 2015 Lean Pathways Inc.

the more bottom-up work you'll see. Andy says there are very few top-down initiatives at Toyota. Senior leaders define True North and the strategic focus areas, and get the hell out of the way.

Strategy Deployment is hard the first few years. We blunder about in the fog, not understanding our current condition. Our hypotheses are weak, our deployment iffy. But if you stick with it, you begin to understand your business.

To their credit, Fox, Harper, McKnight, Penniman, Kwan et al. do everything we ask of them. Madeleine even agrees to take on the Safety and Quality A3—a great challenge. Is she serious, or just playing along?

We agree on six pilot zones, each to be supported by a Taylor sensei. Andy and I will oversee the transformation and provide support where needed.

- Emergency Department—Antonio
- Surgical Services—Bennie
- Cancer Center—Becky

FIGURE 8.12
Carlson's Law. Copyright 2015 Lean Pathways Inc.

- Pharmacy—Elaine
- Imaging—Elaine
- Medical Instrument Reprocessing (MIR)—Becky

The first three pilot zones are major care lines, and the latter three, major support departments. We defer Psychiatric Services, a monster department, to phase 2 of our deployment.

We know from direct observation that the Emergency Department, operating rooms, and related intensive care units (ICUs) are the biggest impediments to patient flow. Imaging and Pharmacy are shared resources and major bottlenecks. The Cancer Center has a high profile and can provide a quick win. MIR has a strong leader and can serve as a learning laboratory.

To support deployment we'll need "boots on the ground." Antonio and the Breakout team will began to build a "Lean Coordinator Network." Network members will attend a series of Lean boot camps and have a personal learning plan. The target is one Lean coordinator in every pilot zone unit within six months. Improvement work will comprise maybe 25 percent of their time. We encourage managers and directors to send their most promising learners.

We'll continue to extend the network thereafter, with a target of one per 100 team members. Antonio will challenge the network to develop multiple learning channels, including monthly workshops, an intranet site, shared Kaizen workshop summaries, and *jishuken** groups. We have to connect the silos and get knowledge flowing.

Concurrently, we launch our "Lunch and Learn" series wherein Grandview team members will learn Lean fundamentals through practice. Leaders at all levels were expected to co-teach with Breakout members. Danny Kaufman develops a multimedia curriculum and learning hub on Grandview's intranet.

John Fox and Madeleine Harper do a nice job communicating True North through multiple channels. The fog begins to disperse. The torrent of top-down projects subsides. We begin to build a management system.

We need an *Obeya*—a big room full of visuals that made our current condition visible. In fact, we need two *Obeyas*—one for senior leaders and one in the Breakout team room.

---

* Study group that focuses on learning, sharing information, and developing kaizen activity. *Jishuken* groups typically focus on major organizational obstacles. In healthcare they might include infection control, medication errors, quick changeover, and integrating new software into existing systems.

"How will we change their thinking?" Andy asked. Teaching Toyota fundamentals to senior leaders will be one of my priorities. If we can shift their thinking a foot, we can move Grandview a mile.

Andy also asked, "How will we engage physicians?"

Roughly half of our physicians work for Grandview; the rest are self-employed. The medical profession is in the midst of a major transformation. Fewer doctors are self-employed; more and more accept paid positions with hospitals.

It's a proverbial two-edged sword. Doctors earn more working for major hospitals and are spared hassles like malpractice insurance and the growing complexity of legislation and information technology. But they sacrifice autonomy and independence, and are often uncomfortable working in teams and in large organizations. Hospital-employed physicians often feel alienated and even disrespected, Harry said. On the plus side, they're smart, dedicated, and understand the scientific method.

After discussions with Dr. McKnight we came up with the following approach:

- Identify three "physician champions" whose role would be
  - Teaching TPS fundamentals to other physicians
  - Attend monthly "physician round tables"
  - Report current activities and answer physician questions and concerns
- Set up a "physicians council" comprising respected doctors from the main specialties. The council would meet monthly and be a clearinghouse for issues physicians had raised. All physicians were welcome to attend and participate in council meetings.
- Add at least one physician position to the Breakout team. Rotate physicians through every twelve to eighteen months.

Andy and I tried to put ourselves in the physicians' shoes. How would we feel if doctors appeared at our auto plants and started telling us how to run our business? We'd never trained in the health professions. We'd never cared for the sick.

Doctors are healers who have dedicated themselves to an ancient and noble calling. We would do our best to understand and engage them. For a start, we would learn their language. We asked the Breakout team and Taylor Motors senseis to do the same.

Andy and I give Gwen and Rachel a progress report at our weekly teleconference. They're pleased. Then we talk about our biggest obstacle: the torrent of top-down projects. I describe its effect on good people like Doreen.

"If we do not reduce this burden," Andy said, "improvement will be very difficult."

"I didn't know it was that bad," Gwen said. "I'll take care of it."

* *

Madeleine Harper begins each day with her diary and fifteen minutes of solitude. She is an early riser; her husband and daughters are asleep. Tribeca's streets are deserted. She begins writing.

> *I don't know if I can manage this way. "Times have changed," Tom said. "You have to learn to lead in a different way. I'll coach you, the way Mr. Saito coached me." But what they're teaching runs contrary to all I've been taught.*
>
> *What am I going to do?*

* *

Tom and Sarah are having dinner at the Blue Iguana. They sit by the big windows overlooking Broadway with its crowds and Christmas decorations. They're taking Sophie and Helen skating at Rockefeller Center this weekend.

"We're getting traction," Tom says. "I've got my energy back."

"Happy to see it," says Sarah. "But let's not forget what we talked about. You have to learn to live in the world. Otherwise, when this fight's over, you'll be depressed again."

"I've contacted a shrink," Tom says. "Dr. Vogel keeps an office at Grandview. He's agreed to see me every Thursday. We start next week."

Sarah breaks into a big smile. "That means so much to me. I know how you feel about shrinks."

"You mean everything to me," says Tom.

Study Questions

1. Describe your organization's planning and execution system.
   a. How is it communicated?
   b. How are team members trained in its elements?
   c. What could your organization do to improve its planning and execution system?
2. What is your organization's purpose (True North)?
   a. What are the "hard goals"?
   b. What is the "heart" goal (*hoshin*)?
   c. How is your organization's purpose communicated?
   d. What could your organization do to improve how purpose is articulated and communicated?
3. How is improvement activity selected and deployed in your organization?
   a. Describe at least three examples each of top-down and bottom-up improvement work.
   b. What could your organization to do to improve its process for selecting and deploying improvement work?

4. Explain Andy's river metaphor using images.
5. What is Carlson's Law?
   a. Do you agree with it? Explain your answer.
   b. How does Andy's river metaphor relate to Carlson's Law?

9

How Will We Change Their Thinking?

Christmas, Hanukkah, and Ramadan. Mass at St. Irene's and at St. Patrick's. Saturday morning jazz and aikido. You're breathing better, Josh tells me, which is something Chiba-sensei might say.

Andy has intuited the key transformation question. Grandview's senior leaders are successful powerful, over-achievers. Their behavior and thinking have gotten them to the top of their industry. Why should they change?

Andy and I have developed a curriculum based on the Toyota House and comprising the following modules. We can add advanced stuff, as needed, on this foundation.

1. Overview—What is a management system?
2. Value and Waste
3. Visual Management and 5S*
4. Standardized Work
5. Quality in the Process (*Jidoka*)
6. Flow and Just-in-Time

* A system of workplace organization and standardization. See Chapter 12 for further details.

7. Total Involvement and Kaizen
8. The Four Rules

Lean is more than a set of techniques; it's a *do,* or Way, like aikido or music. We want to give senior leaders a gut level understanding of the fundamentals, and of their role in Grandview's transformation. We also want them to start teaching the fundamentals as part of their daily "rounding."

People learn by doing. Our monthly three-hour sessions will comprise homework, a short lesson, a *gemba** walk, and reflection. We'll inform the zone of our visit well in advance but won't specify the time. We don't want a show. Each session is built on the previous one. Over time, we hope executives will internalize the system.

We've created learning partners—three groups of two: John Fox and Pinky O'Leary, Madeleine Harper and Arnold Penniman, Carol Kwan and Bill McKnight. I'll be lead sensei.

* *

Grandview lobby, waiting for Madeleine Harper and Arnold Penniman to arrive so we can kick off Executive Coaching module 1: *What Is a Management System?*

They arrive with John Fox in tow. Hope you don't mind if I tag along, he says. We walk over to the Cancer Center, our first *gemba*, and file into the small conference room off the main entrance.

"Welcome, and thanks for your time," I tell them. "We're going to learn Toyota fundamentals and how they apply in healthcare. I'm going to ask questions, draw pictures, and tell stories. Sound okay?" They nod.

"A system is an organized set of parts with a clearly defined goal. We'll learn the methods and thinking that comprise the

---

* *Gemba* means "real place."

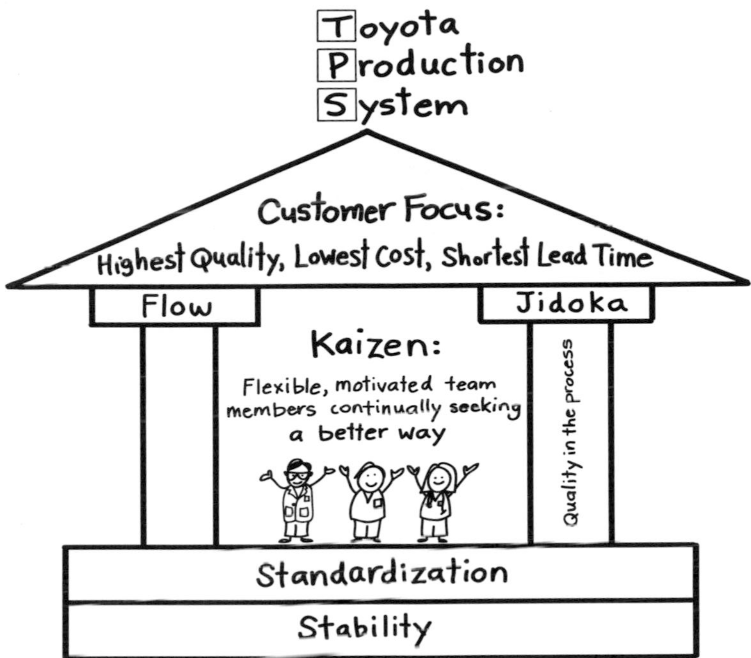

FIGURE 9.1
TPS House. Copyright 2015 Lean Pathways Inc.

TPS* House. They're interconnected and support the goals of TPS—highest safety and quality, lowest lead time and cost."

I sketch out the TPS House (Figure 9.1).

"To achieve our full potential, though, we need to apply TPS in a supportive management system. Here's what it might look like." (See Figure 9.2.)

They listen in silence. Finally, John Fox said, "We don't do anything like this."

"Our approach is more informal," said Madeleine. "Each department is free to manage as it sees fit."

"How is that working?" I ask.

* Toyota Production System.

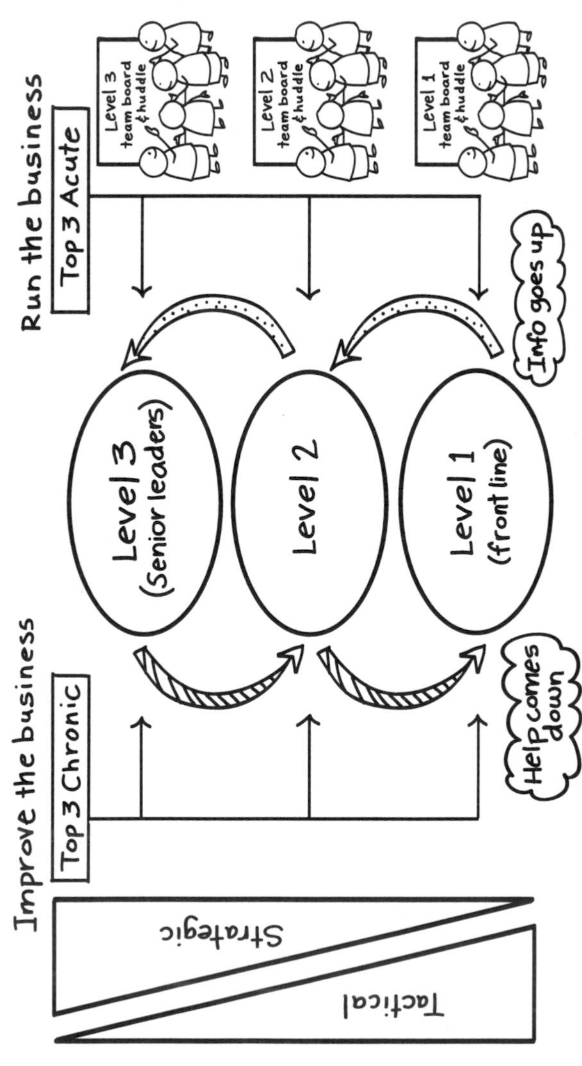

FIGURE 9.2
Our management system. Copyright 2015 Lean Pathways Inc.

"It's about accountability, Tom," Madeleine said. "I expect our managers to manage."

"Who is accountable for the management system?" I ask.

"Why, managers and directors," she said. "We've empowered them. It's their show and their responsibility."

A core mental model was emerging. "With respect, Madeleine," I tell her, "*you* are responsible for the management system. It's your show."

"We'll have to agree to disagree," she said.

Arnold Penniman is absorbed in the drawing. "I really like this drawing. It's how a good football team operates."

"Please explain, Arnold," I say.

"Level 1 presents the front line coaches and players, for example, the offensive line, defensive line, and linebackers. Level 2 means the Offense, Defense, and Special teams coaches. Level 3 represents the head coach and his direct reports."

"Good analogy," I said. "How often does each level meet?"

"Level 1 teams meet after every series. Level 2 meets at timeouts and commercial breaks. Level 3 meets at the start and end of the game, and at halftime."

"Very good," I said. "Imagine a series of gears. Level 1 spins quickly, Level 3 comparatively slowly. Next question: What does each level check?"

Arnold is getting it. "Level 3 checks the overall plan," he said. "Level 2 the defense, offense, and special team plans. Level 1 checks *their* portion of the plan."

I ask Arnold to repeat his insights for Madeleine and John, who might not be football fans.

"What's the purpose of our management system?" I ask.

"Why, to help us get results," said John Fox.

"By doing what?"

"By helping us focus and align our activities at each level," John said.

"And what else?"

Madeleine is struggling. "Tom, we have professional people. I'm sure they do all this."

"We're going to go see for ourselves," I said. "Arnold, what do good football teams check?"

"What's working, and what's *not* working," he said. "That's why you've got the top three problems there."

I nod. "Our management system is there to make problems visible."

"I disagree," says Madeleine. "The leader's job is to ensure there are no problems."

Another core mental model. "Let me suggest a different way of thinking," I say. "Problems are treasure—not garbage to be hidden away. Problems are the process talking to us. Our management system helps make problems visible at each level, so we can fix them." (See Figure 9.3.)

"Physicians are trained in a very different way," John Fox said. "We're supposed to be infallible. Physicians never make

FIGURE 9.3
Problems are treasure. Copyright 2015 Lean Pathways Inc.

mistakes, and we never have problems. To admit otherwise is akin to admitting you're incompetent."

"What's the problem with that way of thinking?"

"You can't fix what you can't see," said Arnold.

"I really have to think about this," Madeleine said. "Let's keep going."

"What's the difference between acute and chronic problems?" I continue.

"Acute problems are recent," John said, "something that just came up, like a player injury."

"Chronic problems are things that we see over and over," Arnold said, "which means we have a systemic problem."

"Where does Strategy Deployment fit in?"

Arnold is soaking it in. "Strategy Deployment is focused on chronic problems, for example, a chronically weak offensive line, or weak scouting. You've got to zoom out and think long term to find solutions."

Madeleine's face brightened. "And what you call 'running the business' means meeting patient needs, and fixing the corresponding acute problems that arise."

"Let me summarize," I said. "Our management system comprises Level 1, 2, and 3 checking so that we can surface problems at each level. Agreed?"

They all nod, Madeleine somewhat tentatively. "Okay," I went on, "who is going to fix all the problems?"

Silence again. John Fox finally spoke. "The front line—that's why you keep talking about total involvement. There are too many problems for the experts to solve."

Hallelujah.

"In a small organization like a football team, you may be able to get away with top-down control," I said. "But in a big organization it's a recipe for disaster."

"I don't think size matters," said Arnold. "A good football coach builds a strong coaching staff. He doesn't try to solve everything himself."

"Fair enough," I said. "Now let's go and see what's actually happening in the Cancer Center."

* *

Dr. Fox was right; they didn't do any of this. Staff, understandably anxious, tried to put on a show. But there was little evidence of a management system. No discernible Level 1 or 2 team boards or huddles, little consciousness of either chronic or acute problems, and no meaningful improvement work. When we asked about the wrong bag, wrong dose, wrong patient problem, people shrugged. There's a task force, someone said.

John and Arnold are embarrassed, as I'd been a decade ago. Madeleine is harder to read. She sends me a text asking for a chat at day's end.

* *

"How can I help, Madeleine?" I ask.

She looks tired. "Tom, what do you see in my management style, in me, that I need to improve? Please be frank."

Can she handle frank feedback?

"I think you're a smart and fundamentally decent person, Madeleine. But you enfeeble your team. You're like kryptonite—when you enter a room, people become weak and quiet. That's not your intent, I know. But if you don't change, our work together will be much more difficult."

Madeleine is silent. "What do I need to do?"

"Learn to lead in a different way" I tell her. "Here's a simple metric. How many units in my zone of control have team boards and huddles? How many units make acute and chronic problems visible, and fix them?"

"I can't answer those questions," Madeleine said. "Maybe I should start rounding again."

"How about you and I start rounding together?"

* *

I've lucked out with Dr. Vogel. He's the real deal, an old school psychiatrist practicing the "talking method." Office in Manhattan, professorship at Columbia, impressive list of publications. Dr. Vogel was born in Prague and fled the Soviet tanks in 1968. It's no surprise he's interested in the trials and trauma of immigration and assimilation into a new society.

I talk about Sarah and the girls, my parents, brother, and divorce. I talk about Andy and how we saved New Jersey Motor Manufacturing. I talk about my depression.

Dr. Vogel just listens. Occasionally, he'll interject a question or insight.

"You're very good at anticipating my needs," he told me.

"What do you mean?"

"You're always on time, polite, you bring me coffee."

"What's wrong with that?"

"Nothing at all," said Dr. Vogel. "But why do you feel responsible for me?"

* *

The second half of the Eagles–Packers game is about to begin. Arnold settles back into his favorite armchair. Nice to see the Eagles in the playoffs again. Marie is preparing a splendid Sunday dinner. Their kids are back from college for the weekend.

Arnold takes a pull on his beer, contemplating the game and the past week at Grandview. Tom's lesson and management system drawing have stayed with him. He knows that the Eagles have just had their Level 3 stand-up meeting. During the first half of the game he watched for Level 1 and 2 meetings. What are the problems, and what are we doing about them? That's what it's all about. It makes perfect sense. Will John, Madeleine, and the rest get it?

* *

Tom and Andy settle into the booth and order beer, Sapporo, and Yuengling, respectively. "We need some quick wins," Tom says. "We have to prove TPS works."

Andy leans back and closes his eyes. "What is your thinking, Tom-san?"

"I'm somewhat overwhelmed, sensei. Grandview is so very different. In our auto plants we have a good understanding of demand. We're able to shape it to some extent and align our production lines to it. We control the rate of arrival and departure of work. As a result we can clearly define and continually improve our processes.

"Grandview Hospital, by contrast, has little understanding of demand. They *can* shape demand in some lines of care but don't seem to know how. Arrival and departure times are random in many care lines. There's a sense of fatalism, and little history of continuous improvement. TPS applies but we'll have to translate it with finesse."

"We have dependent processes with much variation," Tom goes on. "Demand, backlogs, bottlenecks, and queues are invisible. We have to make them visible, reduce variation, and free up bottlenecks. We have to translate and apply TPS with finesse."

Andy opens his eyes. "What is Grandview Hospital's biggest bottleneck, Tom-san?"

Tom takes a sip of Sapporo and mulls it over. "I'd say Discharge."

"Please explain."

"Discharge is the last step in most lines of care," Tom says. "It's a complex process with many dependencies, including the physician, nurse, Pharmacy, social worker and/or psychologist, transport, and the family."

"What is the current condition in Discharge?" Andy asks.

"We don't know," said Tom. "All we know is that our length of stay numbers are bad."

"How can we make the current condition visible?"

Tom is silent again.

"We have to make Target versus Actual visible," he says finally. "That means defining an expected discharge date for each bed, and a Red/Yellow/Green status light. Green means patient is on track, Yellow means the patient is at risk of missing the discharge date, and Red means we have a problem."

"Very good," Andy says. "I suggest Antonio-san and Danny-san put together a Discharge improvement team. My image is a daily Discharge Status stand-up meeting in each major care line. Each bed will be rated as Green, Yellow, or Red. Discharge teams will take action on all Reds. Senior leaders will report out at Level 3 stand-up meetings."

Andy then sketches out a "Discharge Improvement Proposal A3" on a napkin and "makes a video," a series of clear and simple pictures leading to a desired condition.

Tom listens in silence, humbled, and works out the preparatory steps in his head.

Study Questions

1. What is a system? Sketch out your answer using as few written words as possible.
2. Describe your organization's management system.
   a. How is it communicated?
   b. How are team members trained in its elements?
   c. What could your organization do to improve its management system?
3. Describe your organization's Level 1 (front line) team huddle process including who, what, when, where, why, and how.
   a. Has standardized work been developed for Level 1 huddles? If so, describe it.
   b. How well is the standard followed? Attend at least three Level 1 huddles to confirm your thinking.
   c. Has visual management been developed (e.g., a standardized team board)? If so, sketch it out.
4. Describe your organization's Level 2 (manager or director level) team huddle process including who, what, when, where, why, and how.
   a. Has standardized work been developed for the Level 2 huddle? If so, describe it.
   b. How well is the standard followed? If possible, attend at least three Level 2 huddles to confirm your thinking.
   c. Has visual management been developed (e.g., a standardized team board)? If so, sketch it out.
5. Describe your organization's Level 3 (senior management level) team huddle process including who, what, when, where, why, and how.
   a. Has standardized work been developed for the Level 3 huddle? If so, describe it.

   b. How well is the standard followed? Attend at least one Level 1 huddle to confirm your thinking.
   c. Has visual management been developed (e.g., a standardized team board)? If so, sketch it out.
6. Andy suggests the Grandview team can score some quick wins by focusing on the Discharge process.
   a. Do you agree with Andy's rationale? Explain your answer.
   b. Describe the preparatory work entailed in setting up the process Andy envisions.
   c. What are some of the obstacles to developing and sustaining such a process?
   d. What are possible countermeasures?

10

Value and Waste

Late January, so cold Central Park Lake is frozen over and the horse-drawn carriage rides are suspended. For Grandview Hospital winter means hypothermia, frostbite, and pneumonia. Winter means slips, trips and broken bones, asthma attacks, and more traffic accident victims. Our Emergency Department (ED) is doing a brisk business.

* *

Andy and Tom called the Taylor senseis together for a reflection session. What have we learned so far? What are the implications going forward? What changes do we need to make in our approach?

"I am stunned," said Antonio. "I cannot believe what I am seeing. It's mass confusion. There's very little process to speak about."

"It's like the past thirty years didn't happen," Becky said. "It's like they've never heard of Ed Deming, Joe Juran, or Peter Drucker."

"I feel bad for patients," Bennie said. "I see them lying on gurneys in the corridors, alone and scared."

"I feel bad for Grandview team members," Elaine put in. "They're smart and they care. Can you imagine working in such a system?"

“Administrative areas are even worse than clinical areas,” said Antonio. “The IT department is in complete chaos.”

“There are a few bright spots,” Bennie said. “There’s some good activity in parts of Housekeeping, Pharmacy, and Imaging. Medical Instruments Reprocessing is doing good work too. But they’re the exception, and the leaders there are considered to be troublemakers.”

“Sensei, may we have your insights?” Tom asked.

“Grandview team members have not had your training or experience,” Andy replied. “They do not understand value or waste, or standardized work or how to have a daily stand-up meeting. They do not understand problem solving.”

“How do we adjust our approach?” Tom asked.

“I suggest we go more slowly,” said Andy.

* *

Bill McKnight, Carol Kwan, and I are in the Blood Bank for our second Executive Coaching module—Value and Waste. We begin with a short Q & A in a small glass-walled meeting room off the main work area. We look out across the Blood Bank at refrigerators full of plasma bags, tables with the same, technicians, work benches, desks.

“What is *value*?” I ask.

“What the customer is willing to pay for,” says Carol.

“Quality divided by cost,” Bill said.

They’ve done their pre-reading. “Who are the Blood Bank’s customers and what do they value?” I continue.

“The customer is the patient,” Carol says. “Right blood, right quantity at the right time.”

“Any other customers?” I ask.

“Internal customers,” Carol says, “like the ED and Surgical Services.”

“What does the ED need from the Blood Bank?”

"The required volume and mix of blood types, and turnaround time," Bill says. "The plasma also has to meet national safety and quality standards, which cover collection, storage, and use."

"Safety and quality are huge," says Carol. "Remember the contaminated blood scandals?"

"Can we turn these customer needs into simple metrics?" I ask. "Can we track them on our team boards?"

"We can," Carol says, "but we don't."

"In my auto plants suppliers attend the customer's team huddle every day. For example, Paint, Weld, and Stamping group leaders attend the Assembly shop huddle. Assembly is their customer and gives them frank daily feedback. Paint, Welding, and Stamping are expected to address hot spots with countermeasures. I regularly attend to check on customer–supplier connections."

Carol gives me a puzzled look. "They meet every day, and the big boss attends too? How do you all find the time?"

"Short, stand-up meetings in front of a visual board," I say. "Exception-based reporting. 'What's the hot spot and what are we doing about it?' "

"We don't do anything like that," Bill says.

"Not yet," I tell them. "Let's shift gears. Work is activity that creates value. Everything else is *muda* or waste. In my experience, most activity in most industries does *not* add value. Agree or disagree?"

"How do you measure such a thing?" Carol asks.

"In manufacturing it's easy. You observe several cycles of a given process, define each constituent step as value-added (VA) or non-value-added (NVA) and calculate the VA percentage.* It's less than 5 percent in a typical Taylor process and about 20 percent in our best processes.

---

* VA % = VA time ÷ Total Cycle Time × 100.

"Clinic, laboratory or office activities typically have longer cycle time times so measuring VA percentage is a little harder. But it can be done. What percentage of Blood Bank work do you think is value-added?"

"I'd guess a very small percentage," Bill says.

Carol nods. "Not much is happening in here."

"Your instincts are right," I say. "Next question—what are the different forms of waste?"

"There are seven wastes," says Bill. "Transportation, Inventory, Motion, Waiting, Overprocessing, Overproduction, and Errors." (See Figure 10.1.)

"Seven plus one," Carol puts in. "Knowledge is a huge waste in healthcare."

"Are all wastes created equal, or are some wastes more important than others?"

Carol and Bill mull it over.

"You have to triage," Bill says.

"What are the most important wastes in healthcare?"

"Waiting, it's got to be waiting," says Carol. "If the plasma is late, the patient dies."

"Time is muscle, time is brain,"* says Bill. (See Figure 10.2.) "In a Code Stroke thirty minutes is the difference between a normal life and a wheelchair or worse."

"Errors are number two, I think," Carol says. "Mislabeling can mean hemolytic shock and possibly death. We've had some scary near misses over the years."

"And a few hits," says Bill.

They're opening up. I don't want to push too hard on major process and system failures. Well get there soon enough.

---

* Dr. John Toussaint, *On the Mend* (Cambridge, MA: Lean Enterprise Institute, 2010), pp. 34 and 56.

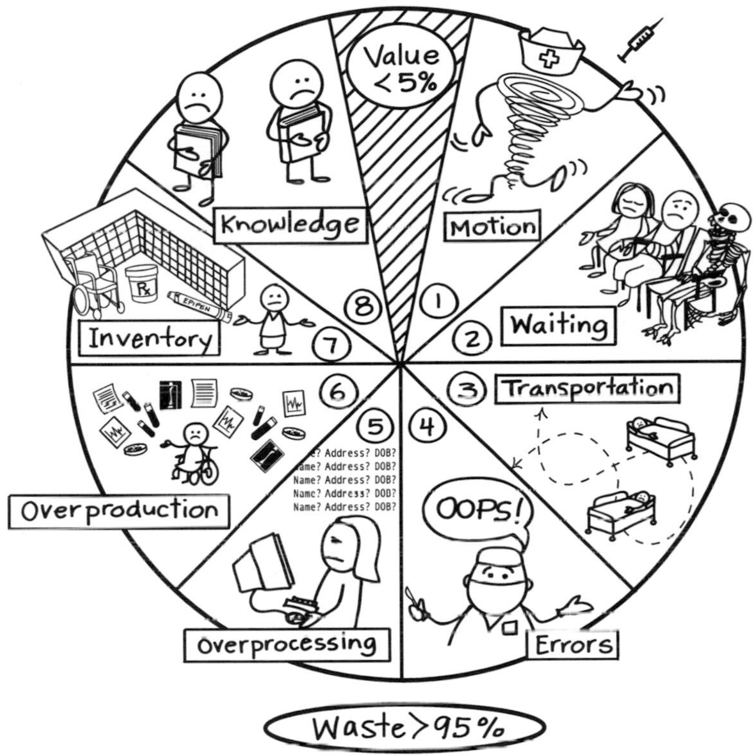

FIGURE 10.1
Value and waste. Copyright 2015 Lean Pathways Inc.

"In summary, not every waste is created equal," I tell them. "Each industry and each zone must figure it out for itself. TPS is much more than a scavenger hunt for waste. It's about getting business results.

"In auto manufacturing, motion waste is a big deal. Poor ergonomics can cripple team members, and the production line. Overproduction waste is corrosive to consumer goods companies. Transportation waste is anathema for FedEx or UPS."

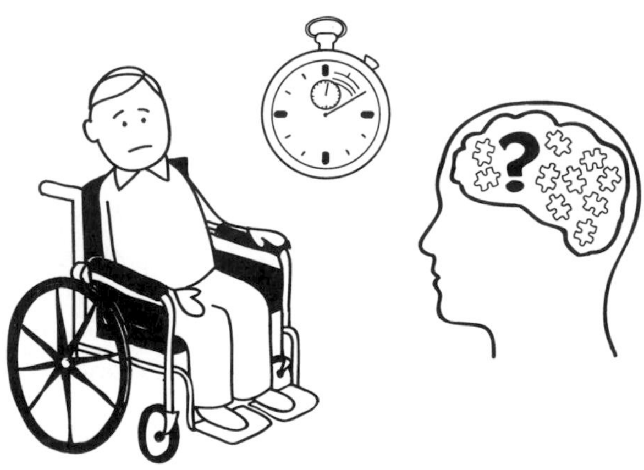

FIGURE 10.2
Time is muscle, time is brain. Copyright 2015 Lean Pathways Inc.

"Transportation and motion waste are a problem for us too," Carol says. "We put pedometers on our nurses. Some of them walk ten miles a day!"

"Not surprised," I reply. "I've also seen bad ergonomics. Small nurses trying to move large patients. No wonder we have so many back injuries."

"Hallelujah!" says Carol. "Tom, maybe you can share that with Madeleine and Arnold. They think our nurses are faking it."

"Overproduction waste is a big deal too," says Bill. "Too many tests, too many drugs and so on. In the past, Medicare and other insurers paid for all of it. Not anymore."

"Let's review," I continue. "Creating value means understanding both your internal and external customers, boiling their needs down to a handful of metrics, and putting them up on a team board. Then you check and get customer feedback every day.

"Work is activity that creates value. Everything else is *muda* or waste. There are seven plus one forms of waste. Not all are created equal. TPS is not a scavenger hunt for waste; it's about getting results. Any questions or comments?"

"I see a big problem," says Bill. "Physicians are trained to be perfect. We *never* admit to problems. But you're suggesting we have to admit to problems every day."

"Problems are *bad*—bury them!" says Carol.

"That's a core mental model in healthcare," I reply. "Shifting it is Job One."

"You can't fix what you can't see," Carol says.

"Is the customer the best arbiter of value?" Bill asks.

"Usually, but not always," I reply. "An important exception is Design. When you're designing new products, services, or facilities, asking the customer is not enough. If that's all Apple had done, would they have developed the iPad? Design is beyond our scope for now.

"Let's go see the Blood Bank. Here's your assignment. First: how well does the Blood Bank team understand value? Second: identify at least one example of each form of waste and possible causes."

We meet again an hour later for reflections and learning points.

Carol is glum. "The Blood Bank does *not* understand its customers. Staff struggle to define value. There are no targets for throughput, turnaround time, or quality."

"There are no Level 1 or 2 team boards or huddles," Bill adds. "Problems are invisible, and I saw little evidence of problem solving."

"What kind of waste did you see?" I ask.

"Inventory," Bill says. "Plasma bags everywhere, and quite a few expired bags."

"How many?" I ask.

"I have no idea," says Bill.

"Okay," I reply. "From here on in, please be specific. How many bags in total, how many expired and so on. Any other observations?

"Very small type on our labels," Carol offers. "O positive and negative look the same."

"What are the implications?" I ask.

They're quiet. "Hemolytic shock," Carol says.

"Nobody in the Blood Bank could tell me how many mislabeling cases they've had in the past year," I add. "They said it was in the computer."

Silence.

"Any learning points today?" I ask.

"To define value," says Carol, "get close to your customer."

"Define value in terms of simple metrics," Bill adds, "put them on your team board and check every day."

"Make problems visible," Carol adds.

* *

All things considered, we're off to a reasonable start. John Fox and the senior team have effectively defined True North, and are communicating it reasonably well. The torrent of ill-advised top-down projects has subsided.

Andy's Discharge Improvement teams have launched. Major care lines are piloting daily multidisciplinary stand-up meetings around Discharge Status boards. Madeleine is beginning to hold senior leaders accountable for Discharge hot spots. Length of stay numbers are beginning to creep downwards.

Antonio, Danny, and the Breakout team are beginning to get traction in our pilot zones. Grandview's mother A3 strategies have been deployed reasonably well there. Grandview pilot zone supervisors and managers are attending two-day practical kaizen training at the NJMM Lean Learning Center. Front line units are developing team boards and huddles and learning Lean fundamentals through our Lunch & Learn program. Bottom-up improvement work is beginning.

The rest of the organization is taking a wait and see approach. Andy takes the senior team through Fukuda's Parable (Figure 10.3), as he did for me years ago at the Iron Horse tavern.

"Fukuda-san is a great sensei, a master of strategy," Andy tells the senior team. "He has developed an image to help us understand transformation. Change is a voyage. But only about 10 percent understand the need and want to be rowers. Most people do not understand the need. They are watchers. A few, maybe 10 percent, are opposed to change. The grumblers will resist change.

"We need to understand who are the rowers, watchers, and grumblers. We must support the rowers and ignore the grumblers, unless they become destructive. Over time, if our plan is good, the watchers will become rowers."

FIGURE 10.3
Fukuda's Parable. Copyright 2015 Lean Pathways Inc.

The only obvious grumbler is Madeleine but she's open about it. Bill McKnight and Carol Kwan warned me privately that there are many others, who are lying low for now.

Danny Kaufman doesn't mince words. "Dr. Brewster is a big problem. He bad-mouths everything we do in Surgical Services. He's not alone. Most docs won't do anything that requires them to change."

"We must stay the course," says Andy. "TPS makes problems visible. We will fix them as they arise."

Then all was pandemonium.

Study Questions

1. Define Value for the following areas in a hospital:
   a. Pharmacy
   b. Imaging
   c. Microbiology
   d. Medical Instrument Reprocessing
   e. Emergency Department
   f. Surgical Services
   g. Housekeeping
2. Pick at least one process in each of the following areas, or in areas of your choice. Observe several process cycles. Estimate total cycle time, value-added time, and value-added percentage.
   a. Pharmacy
   b. Imaging
   c. Microbiology
   d. Surgical Instrument Reprocessing
3. Do a "waste walk" in the following hospital departments or in areas of your choice. Use your organization's waste audit sheet or download one from the Internet and

modify it for your needs. Identify at least one example of each of the "seven plus one" wastes.

a. Pharmacy
b. Imaging
c. Microbiology
d. Medical Instrument Reprocessing
e. Emergency Department
f. Surgical Services
g. Housekeeping
h. What are the most important wastes in each area?

4. Do you agree or disagree with Fukuda's Parable? Explain your answer.
   a. Can you provide a transformation example from your personal experience or reading that supports your answer?
   b. What were the most important factors in the transformation you describe?
   c. Can you suggest any learning points?
   d. Andy suggests that "over time the watchers will become rowers."
      i. Do you agree or disagree? Explain your answer.
      ii. What's needed for the watchers to become rowers?
   e. Why should we "ignore the grumblers" (unless they become destructive)?
   f. Any other reflections on Fukuda's Parable?

11

Moment of Truth

Andy and I are in the Grandview cafeteria shooting the breeze. An emergency text message from Bill McKnight. Come to the Neonatal Intensive Care Unit (NICU) at once. We meet Bill and Carol Kwan at the NICU entrance. It's bad, they tell us.

A prematurely born baby and a terrible error. The child had been receiving both nourishment and medication through catheters and was doing well. But the day shift nurse misconnected two of the lines, flooding the child's heart with infant formula. She discovered her error quickly. But the child was in distress and might not survive.*

The family is in despair. Grandview staff are in shock. The media is running with the story. The nurse is distraught and under psychiatric observation. She's a veteran with an excellent record, and has been going through a hard time at home. Madeleine Harper is going to fire her. She tells the media "accountability is everything at Grandview."

Carol and Bill are grim but resigned. We disinfect our hands and enter the NICU. Tiny frail bodies in incubators, thickets of lines—ventilators, feeding tubes, monitors. Such a hard way to begin life. There's our baby, clinging to life, Mom and Dad

* Thanks to my friend and colleague, Lisa Strom, for this story.

sitting by the incubator. I keep my emotions in check with difficulty.

The charge nurse shows us a typical incubator, catheters, and all the other equipment. She simulates the incident as NICU staff watch. A nurse says to me, "You're going to crucify her, aren't you?"

The catheters have multiple ports. Andy asks the charge nurse to demonstrate how lines and ports connect. Andy and I play with the equipment. Most lines connect to most ports. There is nothing to prevent misconnections—no color-coding, pins, or distinct connections. There's a poster on the wall behind us. *SAFETY IS YOUR BIGGEST PRIORITY!*

I turn to Carol and Bill. "You can't blame the nurse for this. It's a process trap."

"Tell that to Dr. Harper," Carol Kwan says.

"Humans are animals that make mistakes," Andy says. "Critical processes must have error-proofing. The Japanese call it *pokayoke*." (See Figure 11.1.)

"Human reliability is about 99 percent at best," I add. "One error per one hundred cycles. So if we repeat this process a

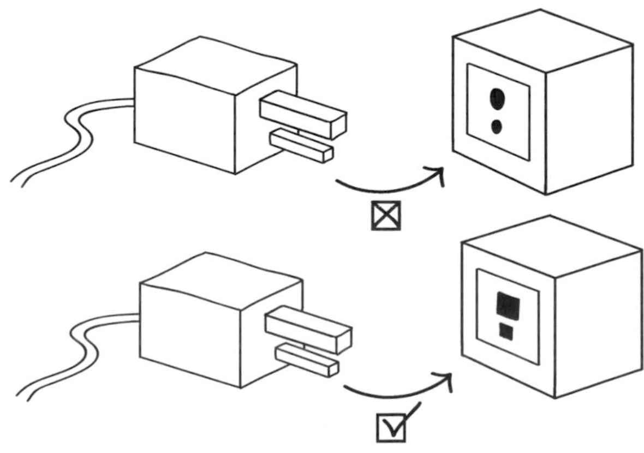

FIGURE 11.1
Pokayoke. Copyright 2015 Lean Pathways Inc.

hundred thousand times a year, we'll have a thousand errors on average. Wrong connections are a common error in manufacturing too. That's why we need gizmos that make errors impossible. "

Andy sketches it out for them in his notebook. "We can start with simple color-coding," he says. "Over time, we can add pins to make the mistake impossible."

"We do this with medical gases," says Dr. McKnight, "both color coding and distinct connectors for oxygen, nitrous oxide, and so on."

"You're telling us the nurse is not to blame," says Carol. "I accept that. But Dr. Harper is still going to fire her."

"We're going to talk to her right now," I reply.

Carol and Bill excuse themselves. I send Madeleine a text asking her to meet us in the NICU. I'm on my way, she responds.

Andy and I put our heads together. The moment of truth has arrived earlier than expected. Firing a dedicated team member over a process trap is contrary to everything I believe in, everything Andy has taught me. It would cripple our transformation. Come to Jesus, Madeleine. It's Yes or No. We break through or wrap it up.

Madeleine arrives a short time later. Andy and I take her through the incident. She avoids making eye contact with the baby's parents, and can barely look into the incubator. NICU staff give Madeleine a wide berth.

We go into an empty NICU room to chat, team members watching us. Andy explains the *pokayoke* concept. "The problem is in the process, Dr. Harper-san, not the team member."

"I disagree with you," Madeleine replies. "Grandview is about accountability."

"Who is accountable for the management system?" I ask.

"How can you hold me accountable for this?"

"You are responsible for the management system, Madeleine-san," says Andy. "Your system is full of traps like this one.

Medical errors, infections, and medication mistakes are to be expected. In fact, if not for your people, things would be much worse."

Silence.

"It would be very unfair to fire the nurse," Andy continues. "With respect, we cannot accept it."

Madeleine looks at Andy, then at me. "You'd resign over this?"

I nod. "It's your management system, Madeleine. I lost my uncle, and, God forbid, we may lose that baby. Sacrificing front line team members may be standard practice. But we can't accept it."

Madeleine asked me to be her sensei. I'm giving her a harsh lesson. It might be our last. "I have to think about this," she says. "Please don't do anything till we chat again." She turns and leaves the NICU.

* *

"Tell me about your family," Dr. Vogel says.

I describe Mama and Dad, growing up with Harry in the Humpty Dumpty. I talk about Mama and Dad growing up as young children in Greece, enduring Nazi occupation, the great famine of 1944–45, and the brutal Civil War of 1946–49.

I tell Dr. Vogel all the stories they had told me. The communist guerrillas gathering up the children, taking them from their families and spiriting them away to grow up as good communists behind the Iron Curtain. Dad's father, my grandfather and namesake, killed fighting them. Dad's uncle and Harry's namesake forced to join the communists at the point of a gun, escaping finally and rejoining the nationalist forces. Then coming to America, Dad and his widowed mother desperately poor, living with Uncle Spiro and family in that tiny Astoria flat.

Dad quitting school and joining Uncle Spiro, God rest his soul, in the restaurant business, learning the trade, saving his pennies. Then meeting Mama at St. Irene's Sunday school, a good girl from a luckier family that had escaped the worst of the tumult. And how they took Dad in and became his second family, especially after his mother died.

Before long I'm in tears. Sorry, I tell him, don't know where all that came from. It's been a hard day.

"You love your parents very much," says Dr. Vogel.

Study Questions

1. Is the catastrophic NICU error described in this chapter plausible?
   a. Explain your answer.
   b. What is the root cause(s) of the error?
   c. What are possible countermeasures?
   d. Can you suggest any learning or reflection points?
2. Tom and Andy suggest that the root cause is in the process, not the team member.
   a. Do you agree or disagree? Explain your answer.
   b. What are the implications of this idea
      i. For senior leaders
      ii. For zone leaders
      iii. For HR policies on compensation, rewards and recognition, promotion, and succession planning?
3. Describe from your experience or reading another serious error in healthcare.
   a. What was the root cause(s) of the error?
   b. What are possible countermeasures?
   c. Can you suggest any learning or reflection points?
4. "Humans are animals that make mistakes. That's why we need error-proofing."
   a. Do you agree or disagree with this statement? Explain your answer.

b. Madeleine Harper suggests that the nurse is accountable for the error. Tom suggests that Madeleine is accountable for the management system, and thus for the error.
   i. Who is right? Explain your answer.
   ii. What are the implications of Madeleine's point of view?
   iii. What are the implications of Tom and Andy's point of view?

12

Visual Management and 5S

The baby is going to live.

We begin to breathe again. Winter gradually gives way to the Easter Parade and Easter Bonnet Festival. Andy and I are still in limbo though. If the NICU nurse is gone, we are too.

Gwen Carter saved the day. "We're not going to fire the NICU nurse," she told the media, "and we're not going to hide what happened. We blew it and will accept the consequences. I've asked the Grandview Breakout team to fix the process, and to engage the NICU nurse."

"You're taking on a big legal liability, no?" I told her.

"Our legal department is not happy," Gwen admitted. "But I'm going to apologize to the family. We're going to learn from our mistake and fix the process."

* *

Madeleine takes several days off. When she returns she asks to meet with Andy and me. "After much reflection," she says, "I can accept that I own the management system."

"What has changed your thinking, Madeleine-san?" Andy asks.

"That tiny baby," she says. "I'm reconnecting with the patient, I suppose. In any event, will you stay with us a while longer?"

Andy looks over at me. I shrug. "Why not?"

* *

Visual management and 5S is our next Executive Coaching module. John Fox and Pinky O'Leary are meeting me at our *gemba*—Microbiology. As usual, Harry took me on a tour there in advance. "Microbiologists are sleuths," Harry said. "They identify bacteria, viruses, fungi, and other beasties in blood, urine, tissue, and many other media. It's elegant, intricate work. Physicians are blind without them."

The process entails collection, culture, analysis, and diagnosis. Beasties are grown in a range of media, and under a range of atmospheric conditions. You have to make them visible, while suppressing common irrelevant beasties.

There's a receiving area, work benches, and a wide array of equipment including incubators, microscopes, fume hoods, refrigerators, centrifuges, and colorimeters. Materials include culture media and plates; slides; and a range of chemical solvents, reagents, and stains. I like the lab—it reminds me of my graduate school days.

Turnaround time and quality, that is, accurate diagnoses, are the lab's most important metrics. The most common error is sample contamination. Grandview's microbiologists are renowned and in great demand, but morale is low and attrition rates high. It's no surprise—there are problems all over the place. How much would John and Pinky see?

There they are. Pinky looks uncertain. John is smiling. "I'm enjoying our sessions, Tom."

Microbiology is a stretch for Pinky. "You must get your hands dirty," Andy told her. "You cannot make strategy from a distance."

I've given Pinky substantial pre-work—an important test. Would she be ready?

"The Toyota system is about making problems visible," I begin. "You can't fix what you can't see. Visual management entails *reverse* magic. Great magicians make the elephant disappear. We need to make the information elephant *appear*."

"We want to satisfy the visual management triangle," I continue. "*We see, know, and act together*—and thereby engage our team members. We have too many problems for the specialists to fix. I'm a broken record, I know, but that's what breakthrough is all about." (See Figures 12.1 and 12.2.)

FIGURE 12.1
Reverse magic. Copyright 2015 Lean Pathways Inc.

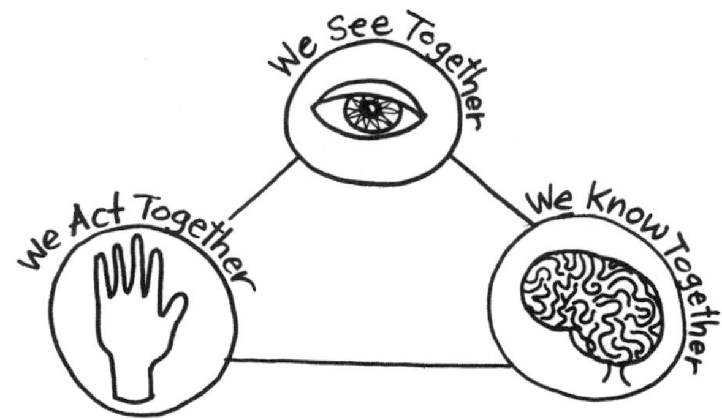

FIGURE 12.2
Visual management triangle. Copyright 2015 Lean Pathways Inc.

I then describe the four levels of visual management.

THE FOUR LEVELS OF VISUAL MANAGEMENT

Level 1—Tells Only (Lowest Power)

STOP signs are a good example. Visual management in many organizations gets stuck at Level 1—signage telling people what to do or not do. As Deming observed, this amounts to blaming the worker, because it subtly shifts responsibility from senior management to front line workers. *"Hey, I told them not to do it!"*

Level 2—Something Changes, Which Gets Your attention

Traffic lights are a good example. "Hey, the light's changed to Green. We can drive on."

Level 2 has more power because it can wake people up.

Level 3—Organizes Behavior

Home positions for tools and equipment are a good example of Level 3. In a surgery, home positions provide a nice visual confirmation that sponges, scalpels, and other equipment are back where they belong—and not inside the patient.

Level 4—The Defect Is Impossible—Pokayoke Concept

Step 1: Go see the process. Understand constituent steps and possible failure modes. Step 2: Install gizmos and/or practices that make them impossible.

Manufacturing is full of *pokayokes,* such as alarms on torque wrenches and electronic lights and safety mats that disable the machine if a team member enters the line of fire. In healthcare, *pokayokes* on gas lines make wrong connections impossible.

As we get better at Lean, our visual management progresses from Level 1 to Level 4.

"Very clear and simple," says John Fox. "But I'm coming to realize that simple is hard."

"I've been trained to think the opposite," Pinky says. "Business school is all about complexity."

"With respect, Pinky, you remind me of myself a decade ago," I tell her. "You'll have to unlearn a lot of things—as I had to. Here's an important lesson. Complexity is a crude state. Simplicity marks the end of a process of refinement."

"Hold on," says Pinky. "Strategy is complex; so is a microbiology lab."

"Correct," I reply. "Our job as leaders is to create clarity and meaning out of complexity. Fundamental principles underlie the most complex situations. We need to bring the underlying order to light. We can thereby make abnormalities and problems visible. Remember, a problem is a deviation from a standard."

"Interesting," says Dr. Fox, "and very similar to what my teacher used to say. Find the order underneath all the data, impressions, and conflicting reports. Engage your whole brain, the rationale and intuitive functions, the prefrontal cortex and limbic brain."

I nod. "Visual management is a wonderful enabler. The brain loves pictures, no?"

Dr. Fox laughs. "Oh, yes!"

"Here's more simple stuff," I go on. "Who can explain 5S for me?"

"5S is a system of workplace organization and standardization," Dr. Fox says. "I'm just repeating what I learned in the Lunch & Learn."

"S1 stands for sort out what you don't need," Pinky adds. "S2 means set in order. S3 stands for shine. S4 means standardize, and S5, sustain. I'm a very organized person—so it seems obvious to me. Doesn't everybody do this?"

"We're about to find out," I reply. "Anyhow, good summary, Pinky. Let me draw it out."

I sketch out a large circle on my iPad. "We have a great deal of stuff in our lab."

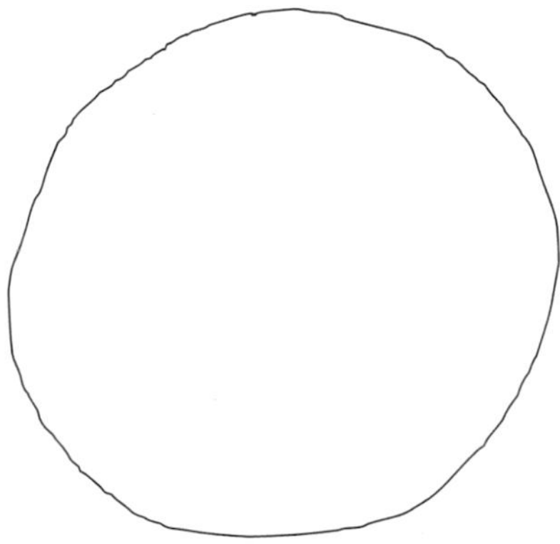

"S1: *Sort* out what you don't need. We decide what's needed and what's *not* needed."

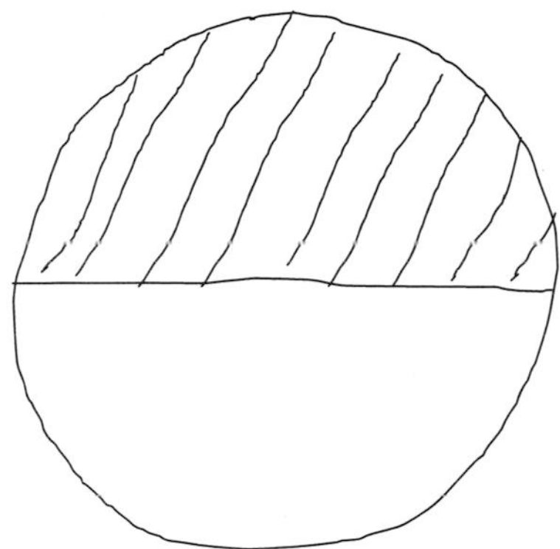

"S2: *Set in order.* We organize what's left."

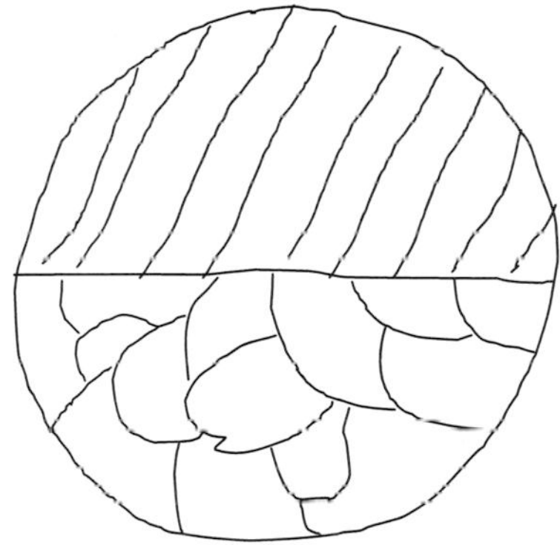

"Now we ask, 'Where is it, what is it, and how many?' We organize along *X*, *Y*, and *Z* axes."

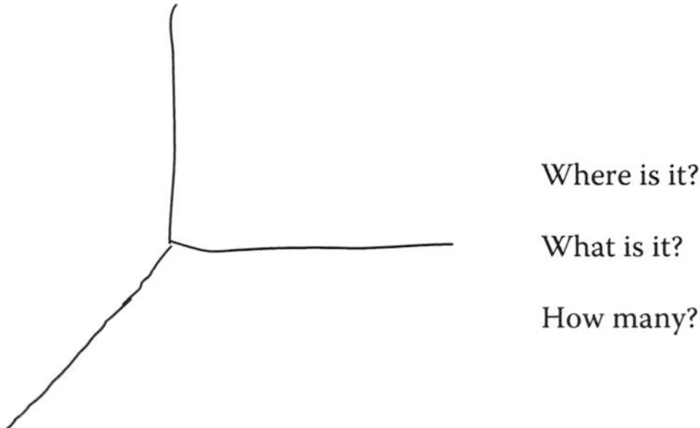

"We use colors and pictures to make it easy to understand," I continue. "Now, we have some space, some order. Next we *Shine* and inspect the workplace—S3. We have to decide who, what, when, and how to clean and what support team members will need."

I pause—are they still with me? "After S3 we have a clean, organized workplace." I go on. "But it soon deteriorates—Murphy's Law. So we need S4–*Standardize.* What does standardize mean?"

"I imagine S4 means standardizing S1, S2, and S3," says John Fox. "S1 standards should help us decide what to keep. S2 standards should address lab materials and equipment, and work areas I imagine. 'Where is it? What is it? How many?' S3 standards should tell us who, when, where, and how to clean."

"Very good. What about S5—*Sustain*?"

"Sustain means doing things that will maintain a good condition," Pinky offers, "5S audits, for example."

"S5 also means training and problem solving, I would think," John says.

I nod. "Now let me introduce a related concept from the martial arts, the Strong Circle. We're most effective when working in the Strong Circle—directly in front of you and roughly three feet in diameter. In effect, it means all the stuff we need is close at hand.

"Now let's pull everything together. The microbiology lab's purpose is to provide quick, accurate analyses and diagnoses. How do visual management, 5S, and the Strong Circle relate to that purpose?"

"Delay and motion are probably important forms of waste in this lab," says Pinky. "So poor visual management and 5S means technicians are looking around for stuff. Lots of needless walking—not good for morale."

"And a higher risk of contamination," John puts in. "Lab techs handle toxic and infectious materials."

"Let's go see what's actually happening," I tell them.

* *

An hour later, John and Pinky are somber. The microbiology lab is a glum, opaque place. No team boards or huddles, and little problem consciousness. Daily and weekly demand is invisible; neither volume nor mix is well understood. Again, it's all "in the computer." Technicians tell us their biggest problem is finding stuff they need to do their work.

Visual management is predominantly at Level 1—exhortations to "Work Safe!" and the like. 5S is at a rudimentary level. We find antique equipment, and ancient materials far past their expiry date. Material storage areas are overflowing and fail to satisfy the three S2 questions—What is it? Where is it? How many? Work benches are messy. There's little evidence of any S4 or S5 activity. We find evidence that team members are eating in the lab, a serious safety violation.

"This is depressing," says Pinky.

I shrug. "What types of waste did you see?"

"Motion and transportation waste," Pinky replies. "Inventory and overprocessing."

"All of which leads to delay and defect waste," John says.

"Any comments on the lab's layout?"

"Confusing," says Pinky. "The process entails receipt of samples, culture, analysis, and diagnosis. But I couldn't tell what was what."

"The layout makes no sense," John says. "They receive samples in the center of the lab. They culture in two different areas, and analyze and diagnose in two others. Samples bounce around like pinballs, which is a big health and safety problem."

"What's a better layout?" I ask.

"How about a straight line?" Pinky offers.

I nod. "Or a U shape. Visual management can blunt the effect of a poor layout, but it's much better to *design* it right. Last question—are team members working in the Strong Circle?"

"They're bouncing around like pinballs too," Pinky said. "Very little is within easy reach."

"What are the lab's biggest Human Resources problems?" I ask.

"Morale and turnover," John says. "Good microbiologists are hard to find."

"No wonder," says Pinky. "Who would want to work there?"

* *

Tom and Andy are taking a walk in Surgical Services. "We are getting resistance from some physicians," Andy says.

"I understand Dr. Brewster has been vocal," says Tom.

"He is unhappy about kaizen activity. Team members want to improve the Standard Order process and the Preference Card process. Team members are gaining confidence and are challenging physicians."

"I understand Dr. Brewster is especially unhappy with me," Tom says.

Andy nods. "He knows you have asked Dr. McKnight that videos be made of all surgeries, and that surgeon performance be assessed against clear standards."

* *

"How are you doing, Madeleine?" Dr. Fox asked.

"I'm shaken up, John," Madeleine said. "The last month has been difficult."

"The media is singing our praises."

"That's Gwen Carter's doing," Madeleine says. "The NICU episode turned out better than anybody could have hoped. But that tiny baby still haunts me. Tom said I own the management system. It's a frightening responsibility."

Dr. Fox nods. "I wish Tom and Andy had appeared a few decades ago. I would have done things differently."

"Well, our numbers are getting better," says Madeleine. "I suppose we're doing something right."

Study Questions

1. Dr. Harper accepts that she "owns the management system."
   a. What specific responsibilities does this entail?
   b. Does the senior leader own "everything that happens in the management system?" Explain your answer.
   c. What is the team member's personal responsibility?
2. What is visual management? Sketch out your answer using as few written words as possible. Don't worry if you "can't draw." Stick figures, arrows, and circles are fine.
3. What is 5S? Please answer with images as well as words.
4. How do visual management and 5S relate to value and waste? Explain your answer with specific examples.
5. Who are the customers of the Grandview Microbiology lab?
   a. What does each customer need?
   b. Translate these needs into a handful of metrics.
6. Do a "Visual Management" walk in at least one of the indicated areas, and/or areas of your choosing. Use your organization's visual management audit sheet or download one from the Internet and modify it for your needs.
   a. Pharmacy
   b. Imaging
   c. Microbiology lab

   d. Medical Instrument Reprocessing
   e. Emergency Department
   f. Surgical Services
   g. Housekeeping

   Summarize your observations and learning points.

7. Do a 5S walk in at least one of the indicated areas, or areas of your choosing. Use your organization's 5S audit sheet or download one from the Internet and modify it for your needs.
   a. Pharmacy
   b. Imaging
   c. Microbiology lab
   d. Medical Instrument Reprocessing
   e. Emergency Department
   f. Surgical Services
   g. Housekeeping

   Summarize your observations and learning points.

13

Standardized Work

Bill McKnight and Carol Kwan meet me outside the Surgery Center for our next Executive Coaching module: *Standardized Work*. We'll observe the Operating Room disinfection process, and assess the work of the Housekeeping dayshift team, an affirming flame in the darkness that is Grandview Hospital's management system.

"Standardized work comprises our current best way to do a given task," I tell them. "In manufacturing, standardized work entails the content, sequence, timing, and expected outcome. Standardized work should be simple, visual, and one-page.

"My wife Sarah has applied these ideas to her kindergarten class, which includes kids with learning disabilities like autism and Asperger's syndrome. Sarah has simple visual standardized work for common tasks like washing hands, tying shoelaces, and going to the bathroom. Here's an example. The child moves the Velcro dot step by step and thereby learns the work content and sequence." (See Figure 13.1.)

"We can't get our physicians to do this," Bill says.

"How do simple visual standards help Sarah's kids?" I ask.

"Builds their confidence," says Carol, "and reinforces the process."

FIGURE 13.1
Simple visual standards. Copyright 2015 Lean Pathways Inc.

"Reduces anxiety," Bill adds. "Kids can be nasty to each other. An autistic child might be terrified of making a mistake."

I nod. "Simple visual standards teach the process, reduce anxiety, and build confidence. But some people say standardized work hinders creativity, especially when it comes to knowledge work like design, engineering, or medicine. What do you think?"

"Some physicians object to 'cookbook' medicine," says Bill. "Dr. Brewster is especially vocal. He says Grandview isn't a factory."

"That's rich, coming from Dr. Hodad," says Carol. "Brewster just doesn't want anybody checking on him."

"Does the 'content–sequence–timing–expected outcome' algorithm apply in say, a Microbiology lab?" I ask.

"Without a doubt," says Bill, "and also in Imaging, Pharmacy, and Housekeeping."

"Let me suggest it applies in almost all short cycle time work," I tell them. "Does it apply in long cycle time work, like Surgery?"

"Great question," Bill says. "I think it *does* apply in a surgery. I want my surgeons to have a detailed game plan before cutting. I want them to picture every incision, every knot in advance. Some surgeons argue standardized work does *not* apply because every patient is different. One has a nice big fat artery that's easy to get at; another has the opposite. They argue that unexpected things always happen and you have to be ready to adapt to them."

"I defer to surgeons with respect to detailed standardized work," Carol says. "But why not use checklists to confirm important stuff? That's what every other industry does. We're in the Dark Ages."

"We have to apply Lean methods with finesse," I say. "We have to *translate* fundamentals so they make sense to users. A checklist is a good example of translation. Let me introduce another important concept—*embedded tests*. They're central to standardized work and the key to building quality into a process. A pre-surgery checklist is, in effect, a list of embedded tests. Sarah's hand-washing example contains embedded tests. At the end of each cycle, for example, the kids hold out their hands for inspection. Timing is a second test—can the child complete the cycle in two rounds of 'Row Your Boat'? (See Figure 13.2.)

"Manufacturing processes are full of embedded tests—throughput and quality tests, timing for each step, safety and inventory checks and the like. As a rule, you want embedded tests for both the outcome—and the process. What are the embedded tests in a surgery?"

They mull it over.

"Outcome tests are almost always clearly defined," Bill says. "Surgeons know what they want to accomplish."

"Process tests, not so much," says Carol. "I was a surgical charge nurse and I've seen some pretty sloppy work—substandard incisions, knots, and sutures."

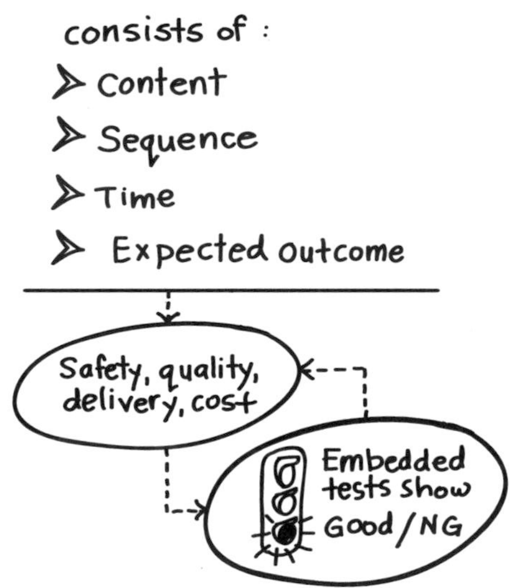

FIGURE 13.2
Standardized work. Copyright 2015 Lean Pathways Inc.

"Are there clear Okay/Not Okay standards for the key elements in a surgery?" I ask.

"I'd say yes," Bill says, "but they're not always visible and not always checked."

"Doctors protect their own," Carol said. "Forgive me, Bill, but you know it's true. Physicians almost never call one another out."

Bill shrugs. "It's how we've been trained."

"In our auto plants process observation is normal," I tell them. "Team members will watch a process for twenty minutes looking for hassles in safety, ergonomics, or quality. We ask them to report and help fix what they find."

Bill and Carol are silent again. Carol says, "We don't do anything like that."

"I know it's a stretch for healthcare," I go on. "But that's where we need to go—embedded process and outcome tests quickly bringing problems to light. Flexible, creative team members always looking for a better way."

"In healthcare we like to hide problems," Carol says.

"I agree," Bill says. "As you suggest, Tom, we need to film every surgery and have a senior surgeon critique and offer feedback to the operating physician."

"We need to go slowly," Carol says. "We don't want a revolt. I'd be happy if they just used our Checksheets."

"Next question," I continue. "Who should develop standardized work?"

"I know you're going to say 'front line team members'," Carol replies, "but we have to comply with regulators and professional bodies. They often give us 'bundles' of stuff to implement, much of which is irrelevant. How do we handle that?"

"Not an easy situation," I admit. "Here's my suggestion. Standard work should be developed at the lowest capable level in the organization, connected closely to the customer, and informed by professional standards and guidelines. In other words, customer first, professional body second."

"I agree, Tom," says Bill. "Some bundles are good, like the Central Line and Ventilator bundles. They're simple and make sense. But other bundles include irrelevant and even absurd stuff. The industry needs to sort it out. If you slavishly implement all the questionable bundles you won't have time for important things. But it takes courage to say, no we're not doing that."

I nod again. "Here's the ideal: team members develop standard work focused on the patient, and informed by professional bodies and regulators. Team members know the work best. Standardized work is their call."

Bill and Carol are quiet. "That makes sense," Bill says finally. "We'll have to manage the interference though."

"Let's go," I tell them. "The housekeeping team is waiting for us."

We make our way to Operating Room 4. Two housekeeping team members and their supervisor are waiting for us. "We're going to demonstrate our OR disinfection process," they explain. They begin by taking us through their standardized work binder. Work content, sequence, and expected outcomes are clearly defined, as is target cycle time. Photos highlight important safety and quality points.

The housekeeping team commences the OR disinfection process. We follow along with the standard work chart. They start with "high touch" surfaces such as surgical tables and carts. They seem to understand cross-contamination risks, and take special care disposing of high-risk stuff such as gowns and shoe coverings. The cleaning cart is clean and well-organized, reflecting a solid understanding of 5S. They comfortably meet their target cycle time of thirty minutes. Lastly, they remove their shoe coverings and the cleaning cart's wheel coverings.

"Who taught you standardized work?" I ask.

"Our manager, Paula Givens," they reply.

"What do you think?" I ask Bill and Carol.

Bill shrugs. "I wish our medical staff worked this way."

"Housekeeping's Surgical Services dayshift team does it all," says Carol. "Standardized work, visual management, team boards, and huddles. You would think they'd get more support."

"Let's go see Paula Givens," I tell them.

After a long walk through Grandview's bowels, we find her in the Housekeeping team room. She's surprised. "We don't get too many visitors."

Paula shows us a Housekeeping dayshift team board and describes the daily huddle process. She takes us through the standardized work binders and training process. They have standardized work for the huddle process too. "Team members run it," she says.

The team board shows Target and Actual for number of rooms cleaned, turnaround time, and number of complaints—for both their regular and "Fast Track" processes (for emergency requests). The most common customer complaints are analyzed and trigger problem solving.

"What are your biggest problems, Paula?" I ask.

Paula looks uncomfortable. "You can speak freely," says Dr. McKnight.

"Capacity is our biggest problem," Paula says. "We've lost 30 percent of our team in the past two years."

"Grandview can't afford to carry fifteen-dollar-an-hour people," Carol chimes, mocking Madeleine Harper's refined accent.

"This is one of our most effective teams," says Bill, "and they've been penalized for it. Paula and her team are stretched very thin. Length of stay and patient satisfaction have suffered."

"I'm not complaining," Paula says. "We've managed to meet our targets by cutting waste out of the process. But it's put a great strain on us."

"You're doing good work," I tell her. "If you ever want a job in manufacturing, please let me know. By the way, where did you learn standardized work, visual management, and team huddles?"

"Twenty years in the Marine Corps," Paula grins, giving us a sharp salute.

"We need to clone you," I say.

Before Bill and Carol leave, I give them some more homework. "TPS is a system; the methods and concepts connect to each other. How do value and waste, visual management, and standardized work connect?"

* *

A few days later, Carol invited Tom to round with her in the Cardiovascular Intensive Care Unit (CICU). Carol wanted to apply what she'd learned about standardized work. Tom accepted, eager to understand the current condition in CICU. His Uncle Angie had died in such a unit.

"What process do you want to focus on?" Tom asked.

"Changing the central venous line dressing," Carol said. "Critical process, often associated with CLABSI."*

"I know," said Tom.

After chatting with the nursing manager, Carol and Tom introduced themselves to a young nurse, Nancy Martinez, who was about to start a dressing change. "Before we start," Carol began, "can you please summarize the key steps in the process, as well as the timing and expected outcome?"

Nancy hesitated, evidently uncomfortable. "May I be honest?" she asked.

"Of course," said Carol. "This is a no-fault process."

"I don't really know how to change a central venous line dressing," Nancy said. "I've never been taught properly. Can you teach me?"

Silence.

"Takes a lot of courage to say so, Nancy," Tom said. "Thank you."

* *

Andy and Tom are having a drink and reflecting on Grandview's current condition. The hospital is making progress, in spite of everything. Problems, such as the absence of standardized

* Center line associated bloodstream infection.

work for changing the central venous line dressing, are coming to light. Team members are less and less afraid. About a quarter of pilot zone front line units have functioning Level 1 team huddles. Most of these units are ready to launch Quick and Easy kaizen (*Kaizen Teian*), which is the door to total involvement. Soon they'll begin basic improvement projects related to Grandview's mother A3 strategies. The water is sloshing left and right, and ever so slowly, finding its way to the sea.

Senior executives are doing their coaching session homework. There's a growing acceptance that "we don't do any of this." Mental models are beginning their glacial shift. Senior leaders are just beginning to apply their learning in their personal rounding.

Andy and Tom are struck by healthcare's isolation from other industries. Andy describes a neurosurgery he observed with the chief surgeon. Tripping hazards, awkward postures, high forces, and severe physical and cognitive strain for the surgical team. "Ergonomics not good," Andy told him. "I know," said the chief surgeon.

Surgeons are in short supply. Injury and burnout rates are high. The chief surgeon said the neurosurgery might last eight or ten hours.

"Physical and cognitive strain mean more mistakes," Andy told him. "At Toyota we would not allow a team member to spend ten minutes in such conditions."

"They've been ignoring me for a decade," said the chief surgeon.

Operating Room ergonomics—another problem in a sea of problems. Andy and Tom know what to do. Prioritize, and ping them off one at a time. Don't get too high, don't get too low. Above all, stay the course.

* *

Dr. Vogel and I are getting traction. We've begun to explore my childhood. Nothing to talk about, I said initially. I love my parents, I had a happy childhood, end of story. But I can no longer deny I have deep and conflicting emotions.

Long-forgotten memories begin to surface. Mama and Dad launching the Humpty Dumpty, the difficult early years, Harry and I helping out as kids. I begin to understand my Dad's anxiety, his panic in those days. Would the business succeed? Could he provide for his family?

"Your father lost everything as a child—his parents, his home, his country," Dr. Vogel says. "Immigration is traumatic for everybody, but your Dad's experience was especially difficult."

"It's coming back to me," I tell him. "I remember his terror, we all felt it."

"What else do you remember?"

I'm silent for a few minutes. "I was the oldest," I tell him. "I wanted to look after him."

Study Questions

1. In a hospital, who are Housekeeping's customers?
   a. What do these customers need?
   b. Translate these needs into a handful of metrics.
2. Define standardized work. Sketch out your answer.
3. How do value and waste, visual management, and standardized work connect? Provide specific examples.
4. Take a walk in at least three work zones in your organization. Assess at least three samples of standardized work in each area.
   a. Is the content, sequence, timing, and expected outcome of the work clear?
   b. Are there clear, binary embedded tests for the expected outcome?
   c. Are there clear, binary embedded tests for the process?
   d. Any other observations or learning points?

5. Tom suggests that standardized work should be developed by the lowest capable level closest to the work, informed by professional bodies.
   a. Do you agree or disagree? Explain your answer with examples.
   b. When it comes to standardized work, how do we integrate the requirements of centralized and professional groups (e.g., improvement initiative bundles)?
      i. Should we implement everything in the bundle? Explain your answer.
      ii. How do we justify *not* doing everything in the bundle?
6. "I don't really know how to change the central venous line dressing. I've never been taught and the nursing SOP is impossible to understand," says the young CICU nurse.
   a. Is this plausible? Explain your answer with examples from your personal experience.
   b. What are possible root causes of such a situation?
   c. What are possible countermeasures?
   d. Why does Tom thank the young CICU nurse?

14

Quality in the Process

Grandview execs are seeing more problems and making deeper connections. They're beginning to understand healthcare is not unique. I'm supplementing our monthly *gemba* walks with articles and papers from leading business and technical journals. Execs no longer balk at the connections between, say, hospital admissions processes and the Quick Service Restaurant industry, or between managing demand in Surgical Services and a stamping plant.

Dr. Harper is perhaps the most changed. People no longer freeze when she enters a room. She's humbler, her body language more open and relaxed. She's even experimenting with Socratic questioning. Not sure what you're doing, Carol Kwan said, but please continue.

Gwen's decision to come clean about the NICU error has turned out much better than expected. The family has accepted Grandview's apology and are not taking legal action. Media pundits are praising Grandview and HNYC for their honesty and humility. Staff are visibly relieved that the NICU nurse has been exonerated.

There are storm clouds, though. Dr. Brewster has begun to talk about Grandview on his TV show. Rachel calls and asks if

I know anything about it. "Let's stay on top of it," she says. "We don't want the Board to get cold feet."

Sarah sends me the link. "I'm concerned," she says. "The mayor is always on Brewster's show. They're buddies."

* *

IT'S THE DR. ZAC SHOW, STARRING DR. ZAC BREWSTER, SURGEON TO THE STARS!

Dr. Zac is basking in applause, mugging for the live studio audience. He bounces over to his chair, trades quips with his second banana, then gets serious. "For healthcare in America," he begins, "it is the best of times and the worst of times.

"I've been a doctor for almost twenty years," he continues, the cameras cutting to a close-up, "and I see a dangerous trend. Our hospitals are turning into *factories*. They're being run, not by doctors, but by *engineers*. And not for the patient, but for *profit*. I think hospitals should be run by doctors, not for profit but for the patient! Don't you?"

The studio audience goes crazy.

Brewster's guest is an aging, dissolute singer who has just returned from Malawi, where she adopted a child and promised an endowment for a new clinic.

"Dr. Zac is right," she says. "Hospitals are not factories!"

The studio audience cheers some more, then the singer talks about her new record and upcoming world tour.

* *

Gwen calls me later that day. "Brewster's a jackass," she says. "Stay the course. I'll deal with the mayor's office."

Later that week, while rounding together, Carol Kwan and I run into Dr. Brewster in person.

"Well, well, well," he says, grinning, "if it isn't Mr. Manufacturing. How did you like my show?"

"Your show is a terrible disservice to our patients and hospital."

Brewster smirks. "What would you know about patients?"

"I know they're being hurt."

"I'm getting tired of your checksheets and all your rules," Brewster says. "This isn't a factory, and I'm not a factory rat."

"You don't like it," I tell him, "you can leave."

Brewster's face turns crimson.

Carol steps between us. "Standards are meant to make your work easier, Dr. Brewster."

"Well nobody asked me about it," he says, before storming away.

Carol turns to me and smiles. "You're a bad-ass, Tom! I've never seen anybody stand up to Brewster."

"He's causing a lot of trouble."

"Know why Dr. Brewster doesn't like standards?" Carol says. "Because now people can see when he screws up."

* *

Madeleine now understands her front line cuts were ill advised. Team member to team leader ratios in our pilot zones are unhealthy—20 to 1 or more. To ferret out problems, we're asking team members to pull the "help chain" and record all the hassles they encounter. But we have to have someone on the other end of the chain.

At our auto plants, the ratio is about 10 to 1. The team leader is expected to answer help chain calls, analyze them, and trigger improvement work. Andy and I have explained the model to Madeleine and asked for more pilot zone team leaders. She has agreed.

Our next Executive Coaching module is quality in the process, or *Jidoka*—a juicy topic. *Jidoka*'s absence was painfully obvious in the NICU near-disaster, and in the oncology drug trial fiasco (which the media has become bored with). Grandview's "task force" is getting nowhere, Harry told me. They'll produce a fat report in six months that nobody will look at. Andy and Elaine Miyazaki aren't waiting. Kaizen work is underway in Pharmacy and chemotherapy bag preparation is a focus area.

Madeleine and Arnold and I meet in the Pharmacy conference room for our pre-*gemba* lesson. "The Japanese call it *Jidoka*," I begin, drawing as I speak, "which roughly means 'I am creating a defect, stop the line!' In practice *Jidoka* means strengthening process *capability* and *containment* with the goal of zero defects (Figure 14.1).

"Process capability is determined largely by the quality of standardized work, and in particular, by the embedded tests that make errors visible. 'Hey, there's a mistake here!' Our goal over the next few years is stability through stronger process standards. And that means embedded process tests.

"*Containment* is *Jidoka*'s other cornerstone," I go on. "Like Andy says, humans are animals that make mistakes. Embedded process tests can reduce error frequency. But to reach zero defects, our shining city on the hill, we also need to *contain*

FIGURE 14.1
Quality in the process (*Jidoka*). Copyright 2015 Lean Pathways Inc.

errors and defects so they never leave our zone. Containment entails embedded tests too, usually of process outcomes. A good example would be a radio frequency identification (RFID) check on a medication cart before it goes out."

"I like embedded tests," Arnold says. "They keep you on your toes."

"Well put," I say. "Big organizations are usually covered in a thick fog. People can fall asleep in it, and smart people can do stupid things. Embedded tests are about wakefulness, as you suggest. 'Hey, we have a problem here. Wake up!' "

"Visual management and embedded tests are closely linked, are they not?" Madeleine offers.

"5S too," I reply. "Think of our material storage areas. Clearly defined home positions, min/max levels, and other visual tools provide embedded tests that answer basic replenishment questions."

"Like, 'do I need to reorder epinephrine pens?' " says Arnold. "Do you know those things cost more than a hundred bucks a pop? We go through them like water. Three million dollars a year! We use fewer than half of them. The rest get squirreled away."

"You're seeing the waste, Arnold—that's good!"

"I see embedded tests in our pilot zones," says Madeleine, "in 5S, on team boards and A3s. But not in standardized work yet."

"That'll take a few years," I say. "Who is the best source of embedded tests?"

"Tom, I know you're going to say 'front line team members'," Madeleine says. "But I struggle with that. Okay, maybe they can design work in nonclinical areas. But our clinical processes are governed by regulators and professional bodies. We deal with life and death and our liabilities are enormous. How can we ask front line people to design clinical work?"

"Auto companies have huge liabilities too. They're governed by tough regulations and professional bodies. Auto manufacturing processes entail life and death. What happens if the bolts holding the steering column, or any other critical items, fail?

"The same applies in aerospace, electronics, food, and other industries. And yet, all these industries involve front line folks in process development. The irony is, healthcare workers are among the most capable, yet you don't trust them to design their work.

"Remember Andy's river metaphor," I go on. "Leaders define the banks of the river. They let the water find its way, keeping a close watch for obstacles and hassles. Arnold, you're seeing a fortune in waste in EpiPens® alone. We've got hundreds of potential leak points. Is a remote team of 'experts' going to solve this problem? And Madeleine, do you really think remote 'experts' are going to solve the oncology drug trial problem?"

"You feel strongly about this," Madeleine says.

"You have to give up the illusion of control," I say. "Leaders control very little. You lead only if team members consent to be led."

"Maybe we should go see Pharmacy," says Arnold.

Pharmacy's purpose is to prepare, dispense, and deliver medications, monitor the patient's progress, and adjust as required. Pharmacists are supposed to do all this as part of the medical team. Given Grandview's silo mentality, how often does that happen? As in the Microbiology lab, the most important metrics are turnaround time and quality (i.e., medication accuracy).

Pharmacy is a pilot zone and about half the teams have Level 1 huddle boards and Quick and Easy Kaizen boards going. I ask the shift supervisor, Robin Jacobs, to show us ideas team members have implemented.

"Here's a nice improvement in our outpatient process," Robin tells us. "We used to have one outpatient queue, long line-ups, and plenty of unhappy patients. Now we have two queues—one for prescription pick-up, and one for prescription drop-off. That triggered another idea. Why not a fast track for priority patients—Emergency Department, same-day surgery, discharge patients, and so on? Both were easy to implement—some signage, communication with patients, and some training."

"What's the effect?" I ask.

"Waiting times are down from thirty-one to twenty minutes, still too high, but better," Robin replies. "We're piloting other kaizen ideas too, such as using the mail for noncritical patients."

"Nice work," I tell her. "Any other improvement work you can show us?"

"Elaine Miyazaki and the Breakout team are working with us on code trays," says Robin. "We're trying to reduce errors and refill time."

Code trays—aka med trays, code kits/boxes/bags, transport trays/kits/boxes/bags, intubation kits, C-section trays, and anesthesia trays—are common in acute care pharmacies. They're used when a patient crashes unexpectedly, and are typically part of "crash carts."

Grandview's busy Emergency and Surgical Services departments mean Pharmacy fills and refills a few hundred code trays each day. The process is prone to error, the most common being missing drugs. Pharmacy has invested in bar code scanning and RFID technology, but it hasn't solved the problem.

We walk over to the drug carousels where technicians were refilling code trays. "This is our first improvement," Robin says. "We've moved the tray refill area right next to the drug carousels. You can see we've also posted tray layout charts to make it easier for techs. Before they had to walk back and forth, and remember what drugs and how many went where. We've also improved the trays—now they show how many per slot, as well as what it is."

"What's the effect on errors?" Madeleine asks.

"So far errors are down about 25 percent. But we have other problems too, such as dirty trays and trays with half-empty medications."

"Anything else you can show us, Robin?" Arnold asks.

"Material storage has always been a big problem," Robin replies. "We're doing a kaizen next week."

Turns out there are four separate storage areas. Labeling is inconsistent. I find vitamin C under V, C, and A (ascorbic acid). Arnold and Madeleine find redundant and expired drugs all over the place. Arnold is mentally monetizing inventory waste. "I'm speechless," he says. "This stuff ain't cheap."

"What's material storage got to do with quality in the process?" I ask.

"Pharmacy techs spend most of their time looking for things," Robin says, "which means there's less time to prepare and dispense drugs. All the rushing around increases the risk of errors—wrong drug, expired drug, wrong label."

"Can you tell us more about wrong labels?" I ask.

Robin takes us to the center of the Pharmacy Department where two large printers are spitting out labels. We look at a handful—multiple labels, different patients, all at the same time. Techs gather and stick them on medications and medication bags. Each bag might have multiple drugs and labels.

"Is it easy to make a mistake?" I ask a technician.

"Real easy," he says. "I double- and triple-check."

"Any improvement ideas?"

"We should print out all the labels for a given patient at one time. And we shouldn't put multiple drugs in one bag. At my last Pharmacy the rule was 'one drug/one bag/one patient.'"

Madeleine and Arnold are pensive at our debriefing.

"You're right," Arnold says. "Front line employees are fully capable of improving processes. We've got to turn them loose. We're swimming in waste."

"Can you see why top-down improvements have limited effect?" I ask. Arnold takes a deep breath. "Task forces are too far removed from what we just saw."

"I like the quick and easy improvements," Madeleine says. "Remarkable how a few simple changes reduced outpatient wait time."

"What did you think of Robin?" I ask.

"High potential," says Madeleine. "We'll have to keep our eye on her."

"Like many of our best kaizen leaders," I tell her, "Robin used to be considered a troublemaker."

* *

Andy and Tom are chatting in their office at the end of the day.

Madeleine Harper walks in. "I'd like to talk to you both," she says. "Mr. Saito, would you round with me in Pharmacy? I'd like to get your thoughts on the oncology drug trial problem."

"Of course," says Andy.

"I'd also like to apologize," she continues. "I know I'm part of the problem. Please be patient with me."

"No need to apologize, Madeleine-san. Management is hard, life is hard."

"It gets easier," Tom says. "Stay with it."

"I feel overwhelmed," she says. "Our problems are enormous."

"No problem, no need for executives," says Andy.

Study Questions

1. Define *Jidoka*. Sketch out your answer using as few written words as possible. Don't worry if you "can't draw." Stick figures, arrows, and circles are fine.

2. Who are the customers of a hospital pharmacy?
   a. What do these customers need?
   b. Translate these needs into a handful of metrics.
3. Take a walk in at least three work zones in your organization. Assess *Jidoka* in at least one process in each area.
   a. Are there clear, binary embedded tests for the expected outcome? Explain your answer.
   b. Are there clear, binary embedded tests for the process? Explain your answer.
   c. How might you improve quality in each process?
   d. Any other observations or learning points?
4. This chapter describes a number of simple changes that lead to significant performance improvements. Are these realistic, or do significant performance improvements require major process changes and investment? Explain your answer with examples from your experience.

15

Flow—Part 1

Tulips, daffodils, and flowering trees—Central Park in full bloom. Grandview's transformation is also budding. More than half of our pilot zone units have functioning Level 1 team boards. Problems are bubbling up and Quick and Easy Kaizen is taking root. Team members are fixing stuff and gaining confidence. Simple things, like the Pharmacy waiting room queue kaizen, or better visual management in the Blood Bank, or layout improvements in the Microbiology lab. We're building our muscles for what Andy called the "endless and eternal journey."

Level 1 team boards reflect our strategic focus areas:

- Patient Quality and Safety
- Service Delivery
- People
- Affordability

Our best pilot zone units have done a reasonable job translating these into simple zone metrics. Their objective is to have at least one significant improvement activity per zone, a stretch to be sure. Some units are doing formal kaizen events supported by the Breakout team. Others are focusing on small improvements. Our underlying message is "get some stuff going, we trust you."

Our Level 3 senior management Obeya is coming along too. True North metrics are fairly simple and clear. Our True North triangle is everywhere. Our current condition is still somewhat foggy but the blizzard of confusing metrics has subsided. Pinky's team has developed a crude Grandview monthly dashboard that is widely communicated. Grandview team members are beginning to understand whether we're winning or losing, and where the biggest problems are.

Our Project Pipeline and Parking Lot are on a rolling white board, sticky notes summarizing the status of each project. Gwen Carter is shielding us from the deluge of Central policy initiatives. We're no longer in the Bermuda Triangle.

Our Level 3 check process has also improved. Madeleine and the senior team have finally agreed to suspend their monthly day-long "Deep Dive." Hundreds of PowerPoint slides, ten hours, and everybody confused. Instead, we're piloting a weekly one-hour stand-up meeting in the Obeya. Our theme is *"What are your hot spots, and what are you doing about them?"*

Each wall is dedicated to a focus area. Key Thinkers report out on a rotating basis:

- Week 1, Patient Quality and Safety—Madeleine Harper
- Week 2, Service Delivery—Bill McKnight
- Week 3, People—Carol Kwan
- Week 4, Affordability—Arnold Penniman

We encourage Key Thinkers to make hot spots visible using dashboards specific to each focus area. Andy's mantra, *"Target, actual, please explain,"* is prominently posted, as is *"No happy talk!"* For a long time nobody wanted to make problems visible and the meeting entailed the usual nonsense. *"Everything is just great, everything is just great!"*

Finally, Arnold admitted to Affordability hot spots, and other Key Thinkers reluctantly followed suit. And so, problems are becoming visible at both Level 3 and Level 1. Level 2 boards and huddles are still weak but that's normal. These entail director and senior manager level huddles around flow and system problems in major care lines. Level 2 leaders' understanding of such problems is still at a very basic level. You can't fix what you can't see.

Grandview execs were initially baffled by our approach. "Why aren't you and Andy freaking out over all the problems?" Arnold asked.

"We want the problems to bubble up," I replied. "That's the whole point. We'll ping off them off as they arise. Our people and management system will get stronger thereby." (See Figure 15.1.)

"Management is a process of discovery," Andy said. "What did I discover is broken today? How did we fix it? And how will we share the learning?"

Arnold gave us a funny look. "You all are crazy like a fox."

Our next Executive Coaching module is both juicy and tricky—"Just-in-Time (JIT)," Lean's second pillar. I ask my senior executive colleagues to schedule half a day for it. Based on discussions with Andy, Antonio, et al. I change the module title to *Flow*. I digress briefly here to illustrate the translation process, essential if we're to disseminate Lean thinking in healthcare.

JIT in the auto industry entails

- Takt*
- Flow
- Pull

* Takt is a German word meaning meter, and is defined as follows: Takt = Available Production/Service Time ÷ Demand. For example, if our auto plant has to fulfill a daily order of 1000 vehicles and we work over two 500-minute shifts, our Takt time would be 1000 minutes ÷ 1000 units = 1 minute.

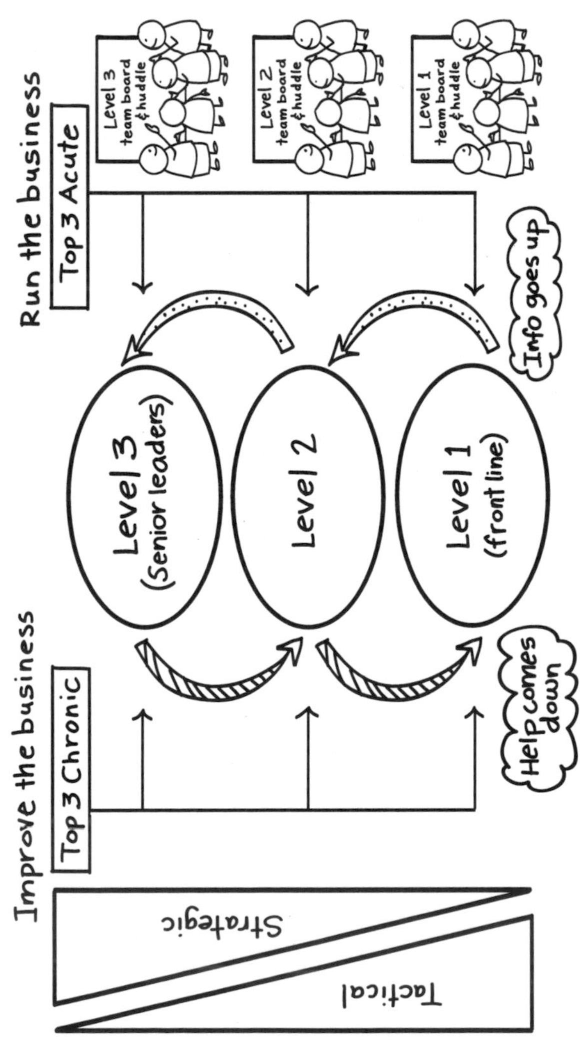

FIGURE 15.1
Our management system. Copyright 2015 Lean Pathways Inc.

How do we translate these for healthcare?

"Flow" requires little translation. Patient flow is the key to meeting our length of stay and throughput objectives. Flow also enhances Affordability and Patient Safety and Quality. (The longer you stay in hospital, the more it costs and the more likely you are to get a hospital-acquired infection.)

Pull is also a straightforward translation. We already introduced the Pull concept in the Project Funnel process with our "Close one, Start one" principle. Pull is also a good example of direct, binary customer–supplier connections, another point we've been emphasizing.

Did Takt apply in healthcare?

In our auto plants Takt provides the drumbeat. Takt is, in effect, our target cycle time. Takt informs standardized work in our Stamping, Welding, Paint, and Assembly shops. Processes with cycle times exceeding Takt are bottlenecks by definition and a focus of improvement activity.

Can Takt serve a similar purpose in a major hospital?

Demand is not completely random, to be sure. Some zones have stable demand where Takt can be helpful (e.g., a Phlebotomy team's daily blood draws or a pharmacy's high-volume medication lines).

But Takt can easily become a rabbit hole in healthcare. An auto plant like NJMM comprises a coherent central pathway—Stamping, Welding, Paint, and Assembly. Demand is fairly stable and we control the rate at which work arrives. Thus, we can plan to make 1000 Desperados a day in the required mix at a Takt time of 60 seconds. For seasonal changes in demand, we adjust our Takt time up or down and make up any differences with a bit of overtime.

Grandview Hospital, by contrast, comprises hundreds of patient pathways with widely varying demand profiles. In many pathways we have little control over the rate at which work arrives. Target cycle times are often determined, not by demand, but by clinicians. For example, target cycle times in high-severity Emergency Department (ED) pathways such as Code Trauma or Code Stroke are determined by doctors, not by how many we happened to get.

Based on such reflections, our consensus is to omit Takt from our teaching for now. We'll introduce Takt where helpful and at the right time. And so, we've renamed the pillar *Flow*.

Grandview's Imaging department, our *gemba* and a pilot area, provides more than 150,000 procedures per year, and has a staff of about 150, including thirty radiologists. Imaging's primary customers are the patient and the patient's physician. Imaging provides services to most care lines and is a major bottleneck. The ED and Surgical Services are the biggest users.

Imaging equipment uses physics to look inside us. There's usually a big team of physicists checking and maintaining equipment. My college physics is coming back to me. X-ray and CT* scans use ionizing radiation, as does Nuclear Medicine. MRI† uses strong magnetic fields and nonionizing radiation. Ultrasound employs sound waves. ECG and EEG‡ measure electrical activity in the heart and brain, respectively. Nirvana for nerds and a potential barrier to improvement. The complex science and jargon intimidate people.

In fact, Imaging is a service business, not dissimilar to the Humpty Dumpty Bar & Grill. Demand is fairly predictable. There are high, mid, and low runners. High-volume services (modalities) such as X-ray images and CT scans correspond to hamburgers and other high-volume sandwiches. Low-volume modalities such as elastography are akin to steak tartare—relatively infrequent but often helpful for marketing.

---

* Computerized tomography.

† Magnetic resonance imaging.

‡ Electrocardiography and electroencephalography.

"Why are we offering steak tartare, Nicky?" Mama used to ask.

"Because Johnny the lawyer likes it and he sends us all his clients," was Dad's response.

Grandview's Imaging department is widely respected, and potentially a major profit center. Like Pharmacy and Microbiology, Imaging's critical measures are turnaround time and quality. Information flows are as important as physical flows. Reports sitting in someone's "in-tray" are a common cause of delay. Safety is a big deal because of radiation and the ergonomics of moving patients around.

Dr. McKnight and Carol Kwan and I begin our lesson, in the Imaging conference room. "Our topic is *Flow*. It's a TPS pillar, like quality in the process," I tell them. "You need both. Flow is meaningless without quality. Quality is cold comfort if it takes forever to arrive. In manufacturing and logistics, we call it Just-in-Time (JIT). Toyota, Walmart, FedEx, and Amazon are all JIT wizards. The Net is full of magical examples. What does Flow mean to you?"

"Patients moving, empty waiting rooms, low length of stay numbers," Carol says.

"Flow means patients moving through the plan of care," says Dr. McKnight.

I nod. "There are multiple flows. Patient flow through the hospital, and through a plan of care. Also, the flow of information, materials, and team members. We're going to focus on patient flow through the hospital.

"Grandview has a large number of care pathways. Each comprises dependent processes and a high degree of variation. For example, each imaging modality entails some permutation of the following steps:

1. Request received and reviewed
2. Scheduling
3. Patient transport

4. Service provision (including patient registration/preparation and room preparation/changeover)
5. Dictation and/or transcription
6. Preliminary report
7. Report verification and release of final report

"What forms of variation is this pathway subject to?" I ask.

"Number, timing, and type of request," says Carol.

"Cycle time, quality, and backlog at each step," Bill adds.

"What types of variation are under our control?" I ask.

"Process cycle time and quality, for sure," Carol says. "We can also control patient arrival rate to some extent."

"Let's summarize," I say. "Care pathways comprise dependent processes and a lot of variation. Some types of variation we can control, others we can't. Patient flow is governed by the laws of Production Physics. You know Little's Law and the Law of Utilization from our Project Pipeline work.* Here are a few more laws:†

Law of Variation: *Increasing variability degrades the performance of the provision system.*

Law of Variation Buffering (Figure 15.2): *Variation in a provision system will be buffered by some combination of*

1. *Inventory*
2. *Capacity*
3. *Time*

Corollary: *Flexibility reduces the amount of buffering required in a provision system.*"

"We normally buffer variation with time, right?" Carol offers.

* Chapter 8. Little's Law: Lead time = Loading/Capacity.

† Walter Hopp and Mark Spearman, *Factory Physics* (New York: McGraw-Hill, 2000).

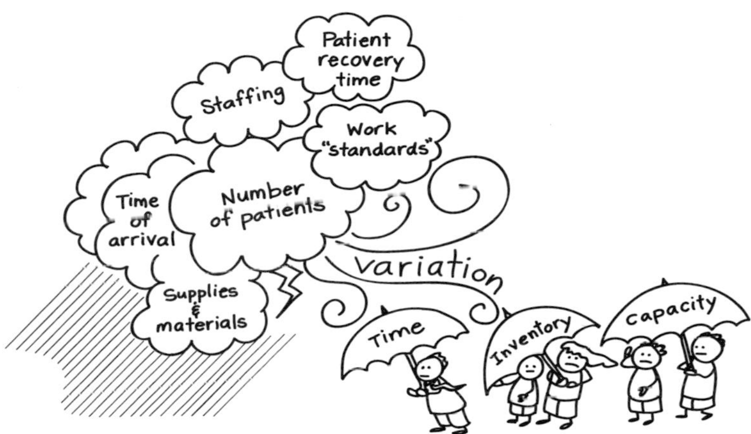

FIGURE 15.2
Law of variation buffering. Copyright 2015 Lean Pathways Inc.

"Hence our length of stay numbers," Bill says.

"How do we buffer variation in acute situations such as Code Stroke or Code Trauma?" I ask.

"Capacity," says Bill. "We've cross trained enough ED staff so each shift is covered."

"Good example," I say. "As we'll see, sometimes we can also use inventory, in other words, patients, to ensure our bottlenecks are fully loaded. The point is to reduce controllable variation as much as possible, and buffer uncontrollable variation with finesse. Imaging has done some interesting work. Let's go see."

Shelley Mathers, the shift supervisor is waiting for us. Like Robin in Pharmacy, Shelley used to be a "trouble-maker." She's gaining confidence in Grandview's changing culture and is a bit nervous having the big bosses in her shop.

"Looking forward to showing you our work." she says. "Our kaizen goal is to reduce turnaround time and improve throughput. We decided to focus on our high runners—X-ray images and CT scans. Elaine Miyazaki and the Breakout team have been a big help. The past three months, report turnaround time is down 24 percent for X-rays and 39 percent for CT scans. Throughput is up—17 percent for X-rays and 21 percent for CT scans. I think we can do a lot better. Don't think we really understand our bottlenecks yet."

"Good progress," says Carol. "What's causing all the delay?"

"Batching for one thing," Shelley replies. "We used to think it was more efficient to build up a pile of orders and process them all together. Elaine proved that one-at-a-time is quicker and better. Have you played the Post-It® Note* game?"

"At our Lunch & Learn," says Bill. "Sure enough, one-at-a-time wins every time. I'm trying to do my notes that way."

"The human mind likes batches," I say. "Grandview is full of batching—reports, drugs, supplies, and tests."

"Any other sources of delay?" Carol asks.

"Patient transportation," Shelley says. "Porters are a bottleneck; we don't have enough to bring patients to Imaging. So our radiologists sit idle."

"Drives me nuts," says Carol. "It's the same with our Discharge process."

"Madeleine is reversing front line cutbacks, including porters," I tell them. "Any other sources of delay, Shelley?"

"Elevators designated for patient transport are being used by visitors and employees on break. People typically press all call buttons and take the first elevator that arrives. Forty percent of elevators open to empty floors."

"Poor scheduling is another one. We found that three of four receptionists take lunch together, leaving the fourth to answer calls, take care of arriving patients, and handle incoming orders. Also, signage was pretty bad, so people couldn't find us.

---

* There are a number of "flow games" on the Net that illustrate basic principles of Flow and Pull. Readers are encouraged to review these and develop their own variations.

Lastly, there was a big delay between the radiologists issuing the preliminary and final reports. They simply didn't realize they were a bottleneck."

"What's happening now?" Bill asks.

"We've fixed most of these," Shelley says, "but I think we're just scratching the surface."

"You're all doing good work, Shelley," I say. "With time, your Imaging processes will stabilize and you'll be ready for the next level."

We thank Shelley and find a meeting room with a rolling white board for the next part of our lesson.

Study Questions

1. Define *Flow*. Sketch out your answer using as few written words as possible. Don't worry if you "can't draw." Stick figures, arrows, and circles are fine.
2. Provide at least three examples of the Law of Variation.
   a. At work
   b. In daily life
3. Provide at least three examples of the Law of Variation Buffering.
   a. At work
   b. In daily life
4. Take a walk through three patient care pathways of your choosing.
   a. What are the biggest obstacles to patient flow?
   b. What is(are) the root cause(s) of each obstacle?
   c. Any possible countermeasures?
5. Why is one-at-a-time processing quicker, better, and less costly than batch processing?
   a. Use examples from your own experience.
   b. Can you suggest any reflections or learning points?

16

Flow—Part 2

I walk over to the whiteboard. "Let me summarize. Patient flow is our Mother Lode. Our care pathways comprise dependent processes with lots of variation. We need to understand how such systems behave. We need to observe, study, and thereby build our intuition. Simulations are good tools."

I fire up my iPad and take Carol and Bill through a series of online dice simulations.* For the next hour we play around with capacity, variation, and inventory. We move these around our simulated system and observe the effect on throughput, backlog, and length of stay. We debrief and I summarize our learning points:

1. The system's maximum throughput rate is the bottleneck rate.
2. Variation degrades the performance of the system.
3. Variation early in the pathway is worse than variation later.

* There are a number of online dice games that illustrate how systems of dependent processes with high variation behave. Readers are encouraged to review these and thereby develop intuition into how such systems operate.

4. We buffer variation through some combination of lead time, inventory, and capacity.
5. Processes always provide less throughput than their capacity.

"Any other reflections?" I ask.

"Understand your process and your bottlenecks," says Carol.

"When your processes are unstable the bottleneck moves all over the place," Bill says.

"Take out variation, especially at bottlenecks," Carol offers.

"Design overcapacity into the system," Bill says. "That's a big takeaway for me."

"Andy suggests a minimum of 20 percent overcapacity* to buffer the inevitable variation that arises. It's much cheaper than buffering with inventory or lead time. Please don't misunderstand, I'm *not* suggesting adding 20 percent more staff. You can't afford that. I'm saying free up capacity by reducing waste and variation, and by cross-training."

"That's an important caveat; thanks Tom," Carol says. "We can't simply throw resources at bad processes."

"Andy calls it 'empty wallet kaizen'," I say.

"Keep your most expensive assets busy," Bill continues. "By laying off porters, we left radiologists idle. That's just dumb."

I nod. "Penny wise, pound foolish. Local efficiency at the expense of system efficiency."

Bill and Carol are silent.

"We do it all the time," Carol says finally. "We're clueless about systems."

"Now let's zoom in," I continue, "and look at how a how a typical high-volume modality, say, CT scans, behaves. We need

* Toyota factories run a maximum of two ten-hour shifts, six days per week—71-percent maximum utilization.

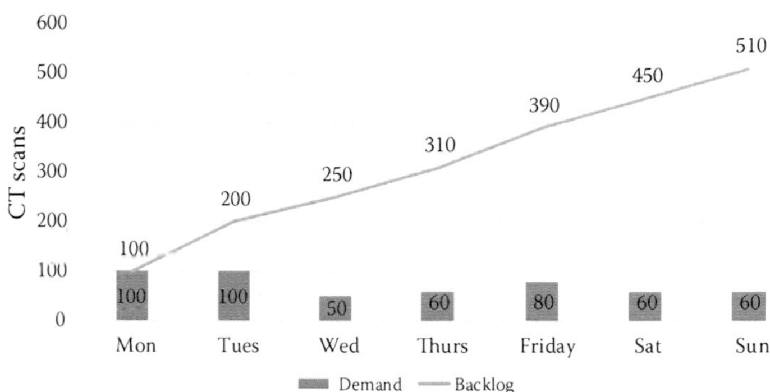

FIGURE 16.1
Demand and backlog.

to understand Demand, Capacity, Actual Work Done, and Backlog. Here's a typical Demand and Backlog profile for a given week,* assuming we did no work." (See Figure 16.1.)

I sketch it out.

"Now let's add Capacity and Actual Work Done. Let's say we've designed our system so that capacity *equals* demand. What happens to our backlog?" (See Figure 16.2.)

"Work done never equals capacity," Carol says. "Murphy's Law."

"Our Backlog grows," says Bill, "patients wait, customer satisfaction dives."

"Now let's increase capacity by 20 percent. Again, we do this by reducing waste and variation, and through *cross training*. We want team members to 'flow to the work.' What happens to our backlog?" (See Figure 16.3.)

"Backlogs shrink, and patient safety, quality, and cost improve," Carol says. "I really like the fact that you can add capacity through waste reduction and cross training."

"We have to teach our front line folks how to do this," says Bill.

* We could also use time as our metric. If a CT scan takes thirty minutes, for example, 100 scans per day work out to 3000 minutes' worth of work.

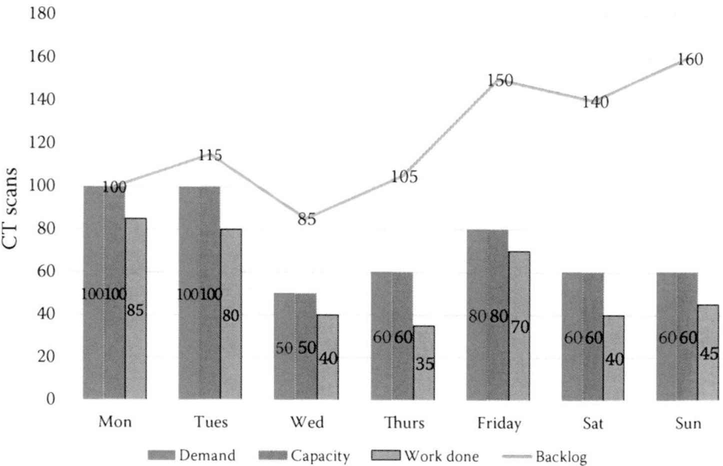

FIGURE 16.2
Backlog—capacity equals demand.

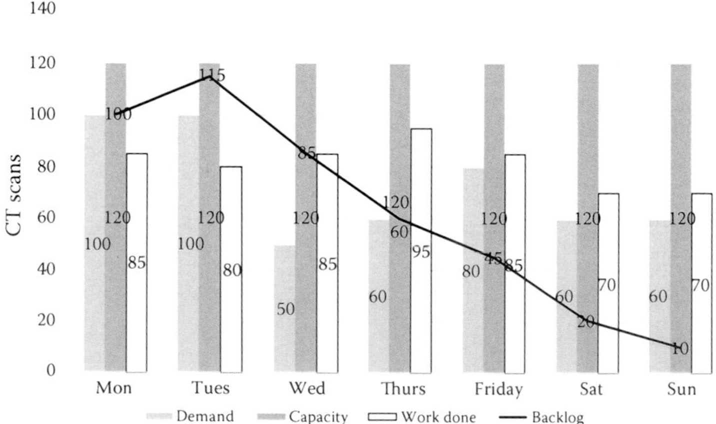

FIGURE 16.3
Backlog—25-percent overcapacity built into the system.

"But first they have to learn TPS* fundamentals, all the stuff we've learned up till now," Carol says. "Now I understand our curriculum."

I nod. "TPS fundamentals are the prerequisite to flow. Without them, it's like pouring water into desert sand."

* *

Tom's Flow session has made a big impression. Arnold came up with a memorable phrase, which he shared at the next Level 3 stand-up meeting. "Lean," he said, "means don't be a dumbass!"

Madeleine and Tom were more than sensei-deshi now; they were friends. Madeleine told Tom about her husband and three kids, their charitable work, and about growing up in a hyper-competitive family. She enjoyed Tom's Humpty Dumpty stories and said she was going to take the family there for lunch. "You're in for an experience!" Tom laughed.

Madeleine dropped by Tom's office one afternoon. "I had a chat with Gwen Carter and with John Fox," she said. "I told them retaining you and Mr. Saito is the best thing we've ever done."

"Thanks, Madeleine," said Tom. "You've come farther in ten months than anybody I've ever seen. I'm proud of you."

"The potential is enormous, isn't it?"

Tom nodded. "We're just getting started."

"But we have to involve everybody," she said. "I see that now. You can't solve Flow problems from a distance."

* *

"How are we doing?" Tom asked.

"What do you think?" said Dr. Vogel, his usual reply to Tom's questions.

* Toyota Production System.

"I think we're talking about the right stuff," Tom said. "I have conflicted feelings about my parents. I love them but on some level I resent them too, especially my Dad. I don't like thinking about it; I feel guilty. I take responsibility for things and situations I shouldn't. I'm driven to achievement and don't feel fully alive unless I'm in the midst of some great battle. I'm not always in the moment, not always present for my family. I've talked with Sarah and the girls about it. They said, that's okay, we love you anyway."

Dr. Vogel looked at Tom. "I suspect you were a super-child," he said finally. "Your brother too, to a lesser extent."

"What's a super-child?"

"Smart, precocious, mature beyond his years, loves his parents, eager to take on their burden. Eager to look after them."

"But that's not right," Tom said. "Kids shouldn't have to look after their parents."

Tom called his brother later that day and shared his insights.

"Dr. Vogel's right," Harry said. "We *are* hyperachievers. I find it hard to slow down, hard to relax."

"Harry, do you sometimes feel resentful toward Mama and Dad?"

"Sometimes," said Harry. "They put a lot of pressure on us, especially on you, being the oldest."

* *

"How am I doing, Sarah?" Tom asked.

"You're a lot quieter, more reflective," said Sarah.

"I think Dr. Vogel is helping," Tom said.

"You're more available, more present. I like that," Sarah said. "You still talk to yourself, though."

"I talk to myself?"

* *

"How are we doing?" Rachel asked.

"Two steps forward, one step back," Gwen replied. "Results are trending up, and the atmosphere is good. On the down side, I'm getting pressure from the mayor's office."

"Dr. Brewster, I imagine?"

"Yes," said Gwen. "He's trying to get Tom fired. Apparently, they've had words."

"Anything we need to do?" Rachel asked.

"Let's stay the course," Gwen said. "I'll handle the mayor's office."

Study Questions

1. For at least one patient care pathway and one business process pathway, please
   a. Sketch out the pathway including all the main process steps
   b. For each step, measure or estimate
      i. Cycle time
      ii. Capacity (e.g., patients, tests, or reports per hour)
      iii. Inventory (e.g., number of patients, tests, or reports)
   c. What are the main sources of variation?
   d. Which of these are controllable? How might you reduce variation?
   e. What's the bottleneck? Explain your rationale
   f. How might you improve flow at the bottleneck?
2. For your chosen patient care and business process pathways, track the following for at least seven days:
   a. Backlog (e.g., number of patients, tests, or reports waiting to enter the pathway)
   b. Demand (in addition to the backlog)
   c. Capacity
   d. Actual work done per day

Summarize your reflections and learning points. How might you improve flow?

3. Tom suggests that we can increase capacity by reducing waste and variation.
    a. Do you agree or disagree? Explain your answer.
    b. Provide at least one example from your personal experience.
    c. What are some of the obstacles to doing so?
    d. What are possible countermeasures?

17

Total Involvement and Kaizen

September—almost a year since Gwen and Rachel tugged on my sleeve. Grandview has changed me, and maybe Grandview has changed too. Dr. Brewster keeps stirring up trouble though. John Fox and Madeleine Harper are getting calls from the mayor's office and from media touts. A few Taylor Motors Board members are questioning our involvement with Grandview. So far, Gwen is keeping the political touts at bay, and Rachel is keeping Taylor Motors Board on her side.

I run into Brewster and his bodyguard, Lester, outside Surgical Services one afternoon. "Well, well, well," Brewster says, "if it isn't Mr. Automotive."

"You got a problem, Dr. Brewster?"

Lester is glaring at me, as usual.

"I have a big problem," Brewster says. "I don't like scrub nurses and orderlies challenging me."

I've had enough. "My uncle died an unnecessary death in a hospital very much like this one. My father almost died. You don't like people checking your work? Then get your skinny ass out of here."

Lester steps toward me. Just then, Bennie Walton turns the corner. "Everything okay, Tom?"

"Just fine, Benny," I reply. "Dr. Brewster was just leaving."

* *

Dynamics, tempo, tone, and more comprise the language of jazz. Jay is teaching me how to put very basic sentences together. I'm also listening to masters like Art Tatum, Bill Evans, and Chick Corea, fooling around, exploring, and weaving their beautiful paragraphs.

Aikido is a language too, comprising the core *kata** I've practiced since I was a teenager. "When your body makes good motions, it feels good." The more I practice the more sense Chiba sensei makes. Core *kata* connect to one another in limitless combinations. "Aikido is endless and eternal." The highest expression of the art is *jiyu waza*, or "free style," which has the quality of jazz improvisation.

Grandview management is learning the core *kata*† of TPS‡ and the language of improvement. We're building our management system on this foundation. To paraphrase Chiba-sensei, when you manage in a certain way, it feels good. We're learning how to put basic sentences together. But we're a long way from free style.

* *

TPS fundamentals need spirit, *ki*, *kefi*, like a sailboat needs the wind. "We can't solve Flow problems from a distance," Madeleine said. "We have to engage the front line." She's come a long way.

But Madeleine is an anomaly. Total Involvement runs against the grain in healthcare, contravenes core mental models, incentive structures, and accepted promotion pathways. Nobody gets rewarded for developing or engaging his or her people.

---

* Japanese for "form."

† Forms.

‡ Toyota Production System.

How to help healthcare leaders to understand the power of Total Involvement? They haven't felt it. They haven't lived through our NJMM transformation.

I remember our kick-off—two thousand people fully committed to saving a broken down old factory. "A lot of people think we're finished," I said. "I don't like that kind of talk. We will save our factory beyond any possibility of doubt." I'll never forget the magnificent roar of defiance, the back slaps and high fives. "We're gonna save our plant, my brother!"

* *

Total Involvement and Kaizen is our next Executive Coaching module and Medical Instrument Reprocessing (MIR) is our *gemba*. Located deep in the bowels of Grandview, MIR is where we disinfect our surgical instruments. MIR's neighbors, incongruously, are Grandview's main kitchen and the morgue. "I'd like to meet the genius architect!" Steve Yablonsky, MIR director, told me.

Steve (Ze'ev) is a PhD microbiologist who, people say, runs the state's best MIR shop. He's a bearded bear, a Russian Jew who fled Odessa as a teenager. "Even before the Berlin Wall came down!" he crows. "They don't let you live, so my family skedaddled. Good thing too—it's even worse now than it was with the commies."

Steve has trained countless MIR technicians and managers over the years. His lectures are legendary for their content and wit. He was an early proponent of TPS fundamentals, going against the prevailing culture and making enemies in the process. He was almost fired several times.

"What do I care?" he told me. "I didn't escape the Soviet Union to keep my mouth shut. The big shots don't like it—too bad. This is the right way to manage. You and Andy are a godsend. I hope the powers that be are smart enough to see it."

Pinky and Dr. Fox meet me at the MIR team room, where Steve is giving a Lunch & Learn on MIR fundamentals for staff and local community college students. We'll follow up with a *gemba*. Steve has fun kibitzing with Dr. Fox. Pinky doesn't know what to make of him.

"Ladies and germs, excuse me, gentlemen," Steve begins, "we are at war! Our enemy is tricky, relentless, and deadly. Kind of like me! Bacteria, viruses, fungi, spores, prions—that's the enemy! Have you heard of flesh-eating disease? *Streptococcus pyogenes*, a microbe we had no knowledge of a few years ago. How about MRSA? Methicillin-resistant *Staphylococcus aureus*—another superbug. We are the front line!"

For the next hour Steve regales us with stories, insights, and jokes. It's both a primer and advanced lecture in microbiology, infection control, and MIR technology. Steve draws out the MIR shop's layout, showing both the clean and dirty sides, and the pathways instruments take (Figure 17.1). "What do you see? Straight lines and U shapes—no chaos! Crazy pathways mean infection. You should've seen this place a few years ago."

Steve describes the MIR process in detail, highlighting both technology and the "nicks and knacks" of the work. MIR comprises

- Decontamination
- Assembly and Packaging
- Sterilization
- Distribution

"Decontamination is the most important step," he tells us. "Soak, wash, rinse—like in a restaurant, except no soap, only detergent. And not any detergent. We are made of protein, carbs, and fat. We need a detergent for each one!"

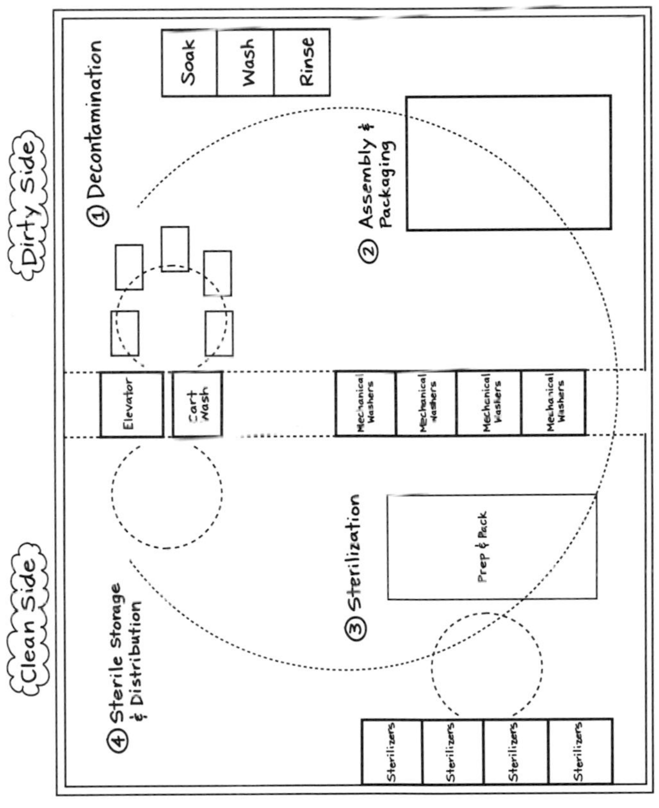

FIGURE 17.1
MIR layout. Copyright 2015 Lean Pathways Inc.

Steve explains the science of sterilization and the relative merits of ethylene oxide, steam, and glutaraldehyde. I'm reminded again there are no boring subjects, only boring people. Steve takes questions, gives homework, and brings the Lunch & Learn to an end.

"A tour de force," Dr. Fox tells him. "Well done."

"I had no idea disinfection could be so interesting," says Pinky.

"Like I said, it's a war," says Steve. "I'm lucky to have such a good team. Mohamed over there, he was head of pathology at the University of Kirkuk. Irina was a surgeon in Kiev. America doesn't recognize their credentials so they work with me, while going to night school. When I hear total involvement, I say, of course! It would be stupid not to involve such people. Wait till you see the ideas they come up with."

"Looking forward to it, Steve," I tell him. "We'll be ready for our *gemba* in about fifteen minutes."

"Okay," he says. "I'll come back then."

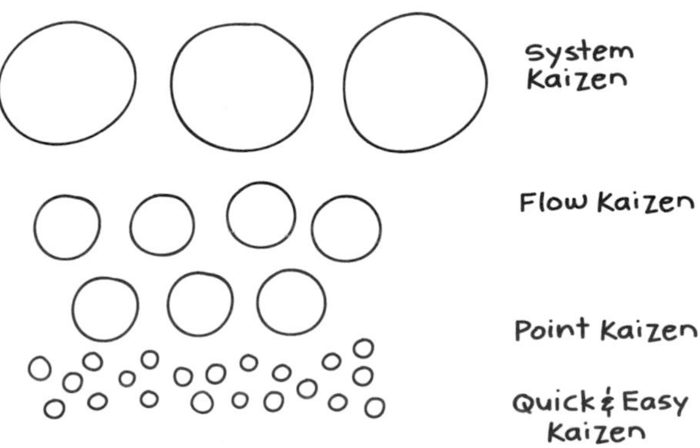

FIGURE 17.2
Kaizen levels. Copyright 2015 Lean Pathways Inc.

I walk to the white board. "There are several levels of kaizen, folks. Who owns each level?" (See Figure 17.2.)

"Team leaders own Quick & Easy, and Point kaizen," says Pinky. "Directors and senior managers own Flow kaizen."

"Senior leaders own System kaizen," Dr. Fox says, "in accord with their authority."

I sketch it out.

"*Point* kaizen entails improving a point in a process," I go on, "for example, improving the sterilizer load/unload process. *Flow* kaizen typically comprises several Point kaizens that collectively improve Flow within a department or care line. Flow kaizen in MIR might comprise Point kaizens within Cleaning, Sterilization, and Distribution that result in overall improvements in turnaround time, quality, or cost." (See Figure 17.3.)

"We learned elements of Flow kaizen in our Imaging *gemba*," Dr. Fox says.

"So Flow kaizen is harder than Point kaizen, I imagine," Pinky offers. "You have to coordinate multiple activities that improve the big picture."

"Level 2 is probably our weak link," says Dr. Fox, "in terms of both the check process and improvement work."

"That's normal at this point," I reply, "The Breakout team is supporting Level 2 with formal Flow kaizen events. Over time, Level 2 leaders will take the reins. System kaizen entails major systemic problems—people, material, information, cost, or supplier management systems come to mind."

"We don't do any System kaizen, do we?" Dr. Fox says.

"Not yet," my reply.

We begin our *gemba* with the MIR team's 1:00 p.m. stand-up meeting. It's normally an 8:00 a.m. meeting but they've rescheduled for our benefit. We stand in the back with Steve so as not to disturb.

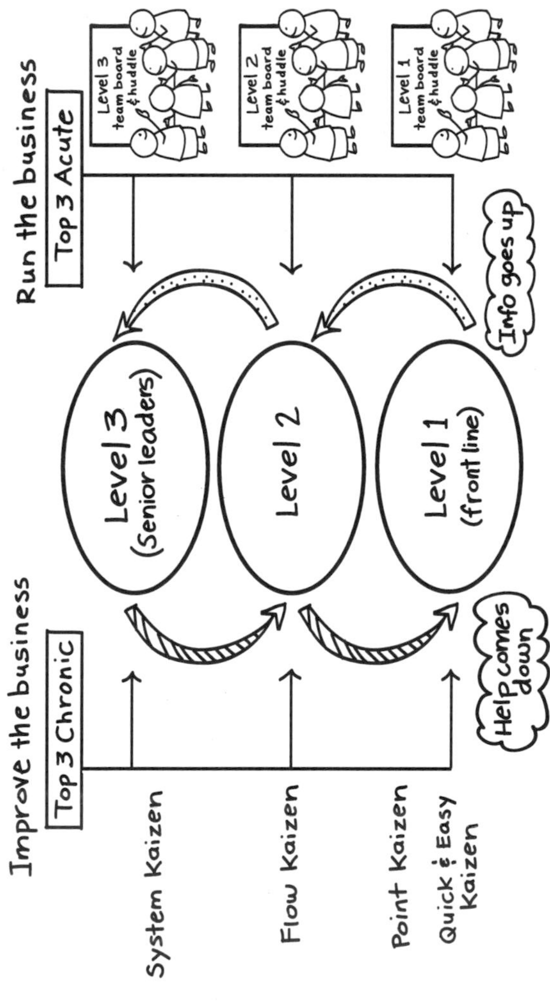

FIGURE 17.3
Kaizen levels and the management system. Copyright 2015 Lean Pathways Inc.

The team leader, Mohamed, runs the meeting. It's succinct, factual, and exception based. The team board (Figure 17.4) reflects Grandview's four focus areas:

- People
- Patient Safety and Quality
- Delivery
- Affordability

The board is subdivided into *Run the Business* and *Improve the Business* sections. The former comprise what Steve calls "daily hot spots," the latter, one improvement A3 per focus area.

For each focus area, there are clear targets and a Red/Green assessment. The team is relaxed and there's much good-natured kidding. Mohamed makes sure next steps and responsibilities are clear, and then moves to the Quick & Easy kaizen board (Figure 17.5).

Again, the discussion is focused and succinct. What's in the idea pipeline? What's the status of each idea? What are next steps and who is responsible? There's a good deal of volunteering.

We chat with Mohamed at meeting's end.

"How do you keep the meeting so short?" Pinky asks.

"We have standard work," Mohamed replies. "Team members usually run it."

"We've implemented eighty-five suggestions already this year," Steve adds. "They're small, but they add up. Let's go see."

We thank Mohamed and put on our personal protective equipment—gowns, booties, masks, and googles. We begin our *gemba* walk on the MIR's "dirty" side, with cart arrival at the elevator.

"Our customer is the operating room," Steve tells us. "They want quick turnaround time, no infections, and low cost. I consider our team members customers too. We're dealing with dangerous

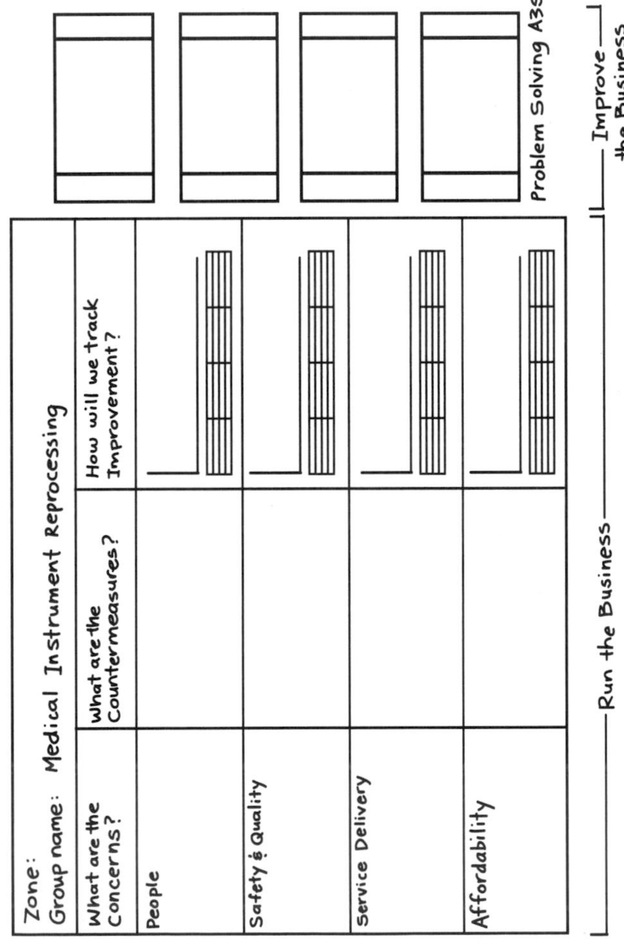

FIGURE 17.4
MIR team board. Copyright 2015 Lean Pathways Inc.

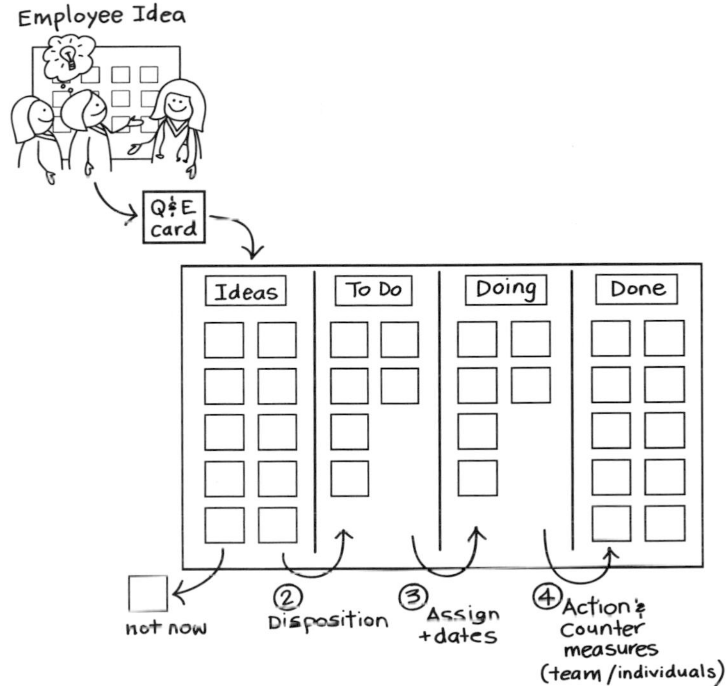

FIGURE 17.5
MIR Quick & Easy kaizen board. Copyright 2015 Lean Pathways Inc.

pathogens and toxic chemicals. If you're sloppy, you'll create slipping and ergonomic hazards too. So our focus this year has been Safety—for the patient and the team member."

Steve shows us half a dozen improvements team members had implemented including

- Splash prevention techniques in the Decontamination area. "Splashing means aerosols, which means pathogen inhalation risk."
- Chemical strips that check the glutaraldehyde solution used to sterilize endoscopes. "Now we know for sure when to change the solution."

- Scanning improvements in the Prep and Pack area that eliminate "wrong and missing" instruments.
- Two-bin replenishment for hard alloy instruments in the storage area (the "Holy of Holies"). It's a simple Pull system," Steve said.

"What kind of kaizen are these?" I ask.

"Point, and Quick & Easy kaizen," says Dr. Fox.

At *gemba*'s end, Dr. Fox asks Steve for his reflections.

"I've always believed in involving people," Steve says. "Now it's a lot easier. Our message is simple. 'We know we have problems, let's make them visible and fix them!' We started with team boards followed by Quick & Easy kaizen. Go for quantity of ideas, Mr. Saito said. Don't worry about quality; it will come. And he was right. People are more relaxed now and their ideas are getting better.

"Becky Johnson taught us Practical Problem Solving. Amazing that an automotive engineer can be so helpful! Our goal is that each unit has one problem solving A3 going in each focus area. Most of it is Point kaizen but we have some ideas for Flow kaizen too." (See Figure 17.6.)

"What can we do to help?" Pinky asks.

"Emphasize True North and the fundamentals," says Steve, "all the stuff Tom and Andy teach—standardized work, visual management, and so on. Make problems visible. Remind people that the problem is in the process, not the person. And come see what we're doing. People appreciate senior leaders taking an interest. Okay, many of them are clueless, no offense. But the fact that you're here today means a lot."

Pinky drops into my office later that day. "Just want to say thanks. You've taught me so much."

"You're welcome, Pinky," I tell her. "Andy and I are lucky to have such good students. I'm proud of you. Please continue."

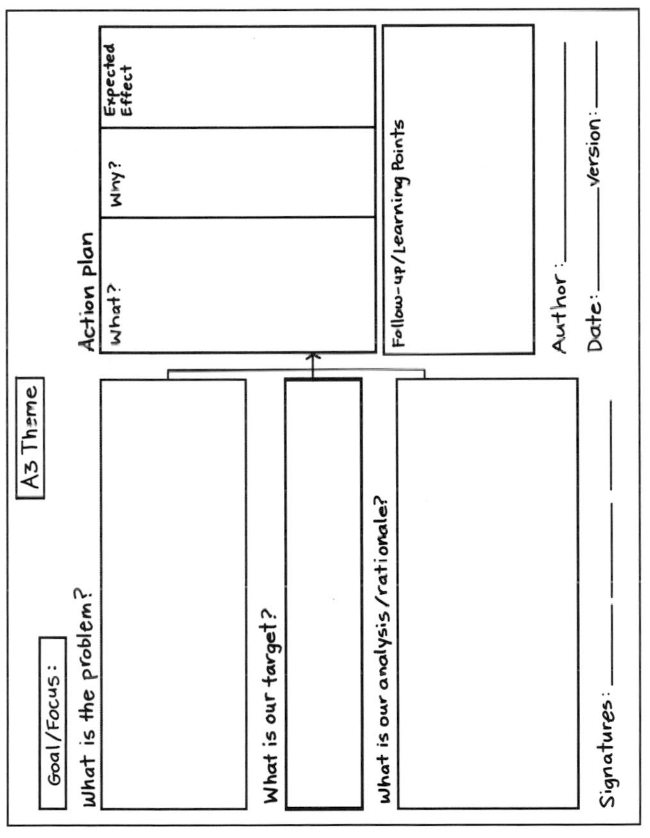

FIGURE 17.6
Problem-solving A3 storyboard. Copyright 2015 Lean Pathways Inc.

Pinky hesitates at the door. "Healthcare is very political," she says. "I hope the mayor's office, and all the others, leave us alone. We're doing better than we ever have."

Pinky's parents are members of New York's business and political elite. She knows how the game is played.

"Let's see what happens," I tell her.

* *

Our MIR *gemba* triggers an epiphany in Dr. Fox. "I am the problem, we are the problem," he tells the senior management team. "I spent a decade in the hermetically sealed tube known as medical school and residency. I've been taught to be imperious and infallible. I've learned 'white coat management.' *Do what I say, and do it quick. No questions, the doctor knows everything.* It's absurd but there it is. And that's how I still manage. I am the problem. We are the problem."

The words hang there, a rebuke and a challenge. Not everybody is happy to hear them.

Our transformation is frail, vulnerable. The hospital is full of grumblers. The mayor's office and state and federal agencies are run by command and control types who believe they can "fix healthcare" from afar. The touts further their careers, thereby, at the expense of the patients and the hospital.

We've been lucky so far. Gwen Carter is keeping the politicos at bay. Grandview's senior leaders are for the most part open and engaged. It's a good incubator for improvement. But things can easily unravel. Take away Gwen Carter, Dr. Fox, or Dr. Harper and we're in trouble.

* *

Dr. Vogel and I are also in uncomfortable territory. Like Andy, Dr. Vogel uses a form of Socratic questioning and provides few answers. He suggests the dots; I have to connect them. For a long time I haven't wanted to. Our sessions comprise Dr. Vogel looking at me while I deny, deny, deny. He finally gives me a nudge. "Have you heard of Atlas?"

Greek mythology: Atlas sided with the Titans against Zeus and the Olympian gods. Zeus punished Atlas by condemning him to hold the sky and heavens on his shoulders for eternity.

I'm silent for a long time. I see a precocious kid running around the family restaurant, a kid who loves his anxious parents and wants to look after them, taking on burdens that aren't his to carry. I see the kid growing up and compulsively doing what he's learned to do. The kid becomes successful. He is praised and rewarded for all the burdens he takes on. But in the process he often neglects his own needs and those of his family, and forgets how to enjoy life.

I feel thick, heavy, and as if I'm meeting a stranger (Figure 17.7).

"Say hello to yourself," says Dr. Vogel.

* *

That weekend I drop into the Humpty Dumpty after aikido class. I want to talk to Mama about the early years.

"Things were very difficult, agape mou," she tells me. "We were very poor and didn't know if the business would survive. The economy was bad. The city was a mess. There was crime and garbage everywhere. It was very hard on your father. He was so worried, he was like a child."

We can see Dad through the serving window clowning around.

"I remember one time," Mama says, "I hear a smash and you come in holding all these coins. These are for you, Mama, you said. You broke your piggy bank for us. You've always been like that, chriso mou."

* *

I share my epiphany with Andy. We're sitting in the Blue Iguana patio enjoying the sunlight. Later I'm taking Sarah to

FIGURE 17.7
Tom's epiphany. Copyright 2015 Lean Pathways Inc.

dinner at her favorite restaurant. She says she has a surprise for me.

"I am the same, Tom-san," Andy says. "It has taken me a long time to understand."

Andy paid an awful price for his inattention. Though his friend, Mrs. Yamamoto, is a fine companion, Shizuko's loss would always pain him. Andy's words haunt me. "She was my wife, my best friend, and biggest supporter. But when she needed me I was not there."

Would I make the same mistake as my sensei?

"You are much more aware, Tom-san. When I was young our only thought was to help rebuild Japan. We worked very long hours and did good work, but did we live our lives well? I don't know."

"You achieved a miracle, sensei. With honor and grace."

"The price was very high, Tom-san."

We're silent. Andy and his generation were dealt a tough hand. Poverty, humiliation, anxiety, and guilt. They did their very best, and they changed the world.

Am I Atlas, condemned to carry the sky and heavens on my shoulders? Am I responsible for everything that happens at Grandview or Taylor Motors? Am I responsible for Uncle Angie, or for my Dad's traumatic childhood?

* *

"We're going to Grand Cayman," Sarah says. "No ifs, maybes, or buts! Sophie and Helen are coming too. I've worked it all out with Teal. Five days in the sun, snorkeling and relaxing."

Tom laughs. "I guess Grandview will survive without me."

A few days later Tom and Sarah are walking in the sand after a fine dinner. Sophie and Helen are running ahead, skipping stones and laughing. The sun has set and the stars are coming out.

Tom looks up at the night sky, thinking "I don't have to carry you anymore." Later that evening Sarah tells him he's going to be a Dad again.

Study Questions

1. With respect to Total Involvement, what's the role of
    a. The senior executive?
    b. The department or zone leader?
    c. The team leader?

2. Identify at least five channels (e.g., suggestion systems, formal kaizen workshops, etc.) through which we can involve front-line team members in running and improving the business.
   a. What are relative strengths and weaknesses of each channel?
   b. In your experience, which channels are the most effective, and why?
3. How well does your organization involve team members in running and improving the business? Explain your answer.
   a. What are the main channels of involvement?
   b. What can your organization do to improve team member involvement?
4. From your experience, describe an organization that excels in team member involvement.
   a. What makes the organization so good at involving people?
   b. What benefits does the organization gain thereby?
5. From your experience provide at least one example of
   a. Quick & Easy kaizen
   b. Point kaizen
   c. Flow kaizen
   d. System kaizen
6. How well does your organization practice each level of kaizen? Explain your answer with examples. What might your organization do to improve?

18

The Four Rules

Autumn again, leaves tracing lazing pirouettes, Central Park, a yellow carpet. Another month and we'll have our year-end review. We're on track for double-digit improvement in our main metrics. Grandview, and even Taylor Motors are getting positive media coverage. Our YouTube videos are going viral. Everybody is happy.

Don't get too high, don't get too low, Andy and I tell them. We've barely started.

Dr. Brewster's TV show attacks, though more intense, are now just a distraction. Brewster lobbied hard against Dr. McKnight's decision to video all surgeries. He unsuccessfully opposed the new rules around decontamination. People are beginning to tune him out. I notice Lester hanging around more—moral support, I suppose.

* *

Senior executives have gained a basic understanding of TPS* fundamentals. Our next Executive Coaching module will be the Four Rules, which bring the TPS methods and thinking into sharp relief.

---

* Toyota Production System.

Our friend Dr. Sam Sparrow was the first to articulate* the Four Rules. Sam is a Boston Institute of Technology professor whose specialty is system dynamics, and in particular, how complex systems fail—and succeed. Sam met Andy years ago while working on his doctorate. Sam was a great help during the Chloe launch and we've stayed in touch.

Our *gemba* is Grandview's most complex zone and biggest bottleneck—the Emergency Department (ED). Andy and Antonio Villarreal have been supporting ED improvement work. I've asked Andy to join us for our go see.

The ED chessboard is daunting:

- More than 105,000 ED visits per year
- 70,000 square feet of clinical space with 20 examining beds
- Designated hospital for neurosurgical trauma, poisonings, and amputations requiring reimplantation
- All major specialties available 24 hours a day
- Trauma suite for critically ill patients in need of rapid resuscitation
- ED Intensive Care Unit for critically ill patients

The ED team is beginning to understand their current condition. They've stratified ED visits according to the Emergency Severity Index (ESI; Figure 18.1) and found *only 16 percent* are urgent. About 55 percent are nonacute and do not require emergency attention. These comprise all Level 4 and 5 patients (39 percent) and almost half of Level 3 patients (Figure 18.2). Turns out ED demand is *not* random—there are daily and seasonal patterns (Figures 18.3 and 18.4).

* Pascal Dennis, *The Remedy—Bringing Lean Out of the Factory to Transform the Entire Organization* (New York: John Wiley & Sons, 2010), Chapter 7.

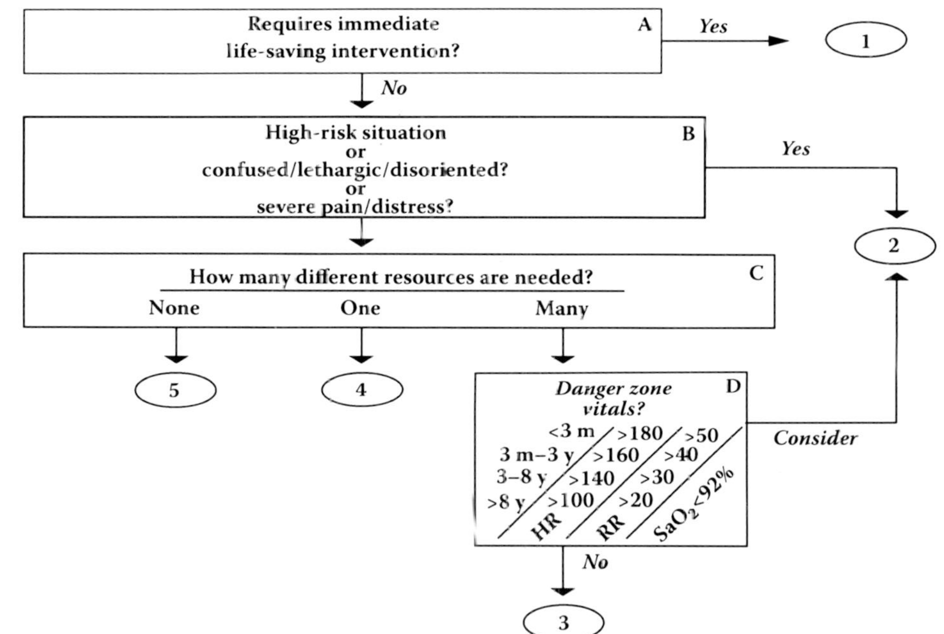

FIGURE 18.1
Emergency Severity Index. A five-level ED triage algorithm that provides clinically relevant stratification of patients into five groups from 1 (most urgent) to 5 (least urgent). HR, heart rate; RR, respiratory rate; SaO_2, blood oxygen saturation rate.

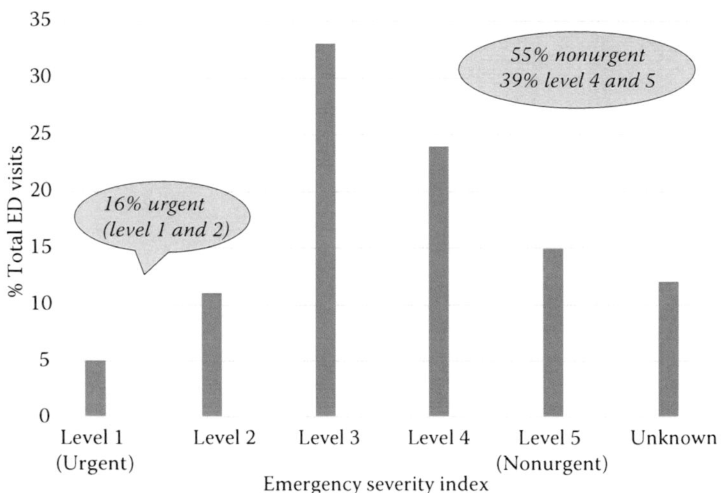

FIGURE 18.2
Grandview ED visits by severity.

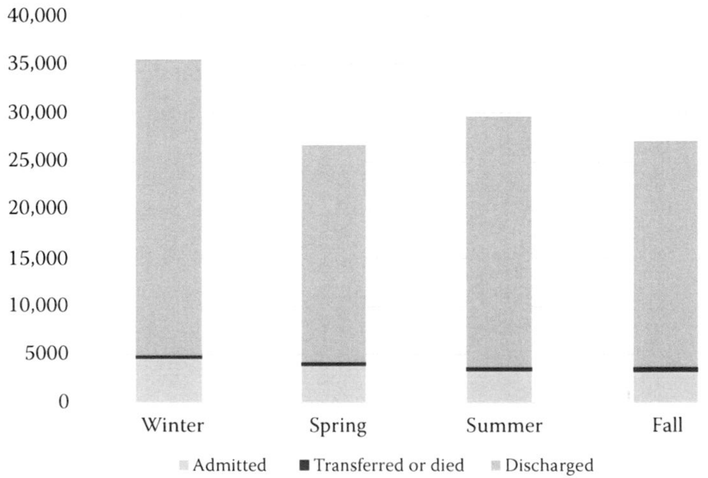

FIGURE 18.3
Grandview ED admission status by season.

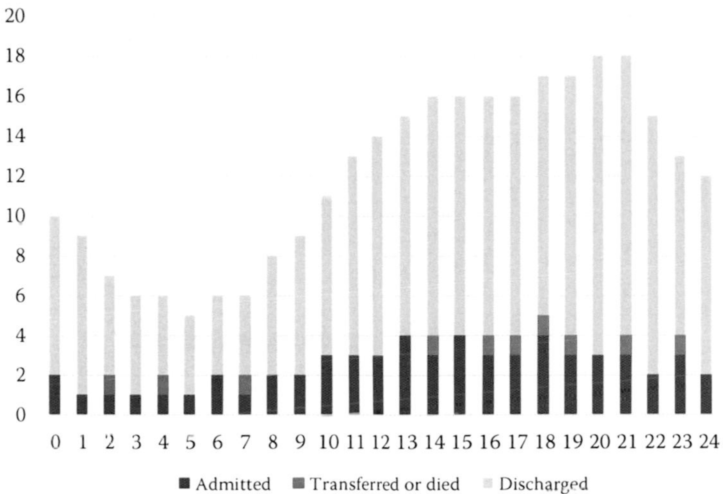

FIGURE 18.4
Grandview ED admission status by 24-hour clock.

Our improvement focus is length of stay (LOS) and walk-aways (Figures 18.5 and 18.6). Median and Average LOS data strongly suggest a bias toward longer LOS episodes, the ones that drive people crazy. Excessive LOS numbers correspond to overutilization of core servers (nurses, doctors, and beds).

We're prone to it. Our shift schedules do *not* correspond to daily demand. We're over-staffed when we *don't* need people, and understaffed when we *do*.

Madeleine and Arnold and I meet in the ED conference room. "We've learned core TPS hardware," I tell them. "Now we're going to learn the software. Let's go back in time to Grandview Hospital in 1950. What do the ED, Surgery, Oncology, and all the care lines look like? What do the Pharmacy, Imagining, Microbiology, and other support groups look like?"

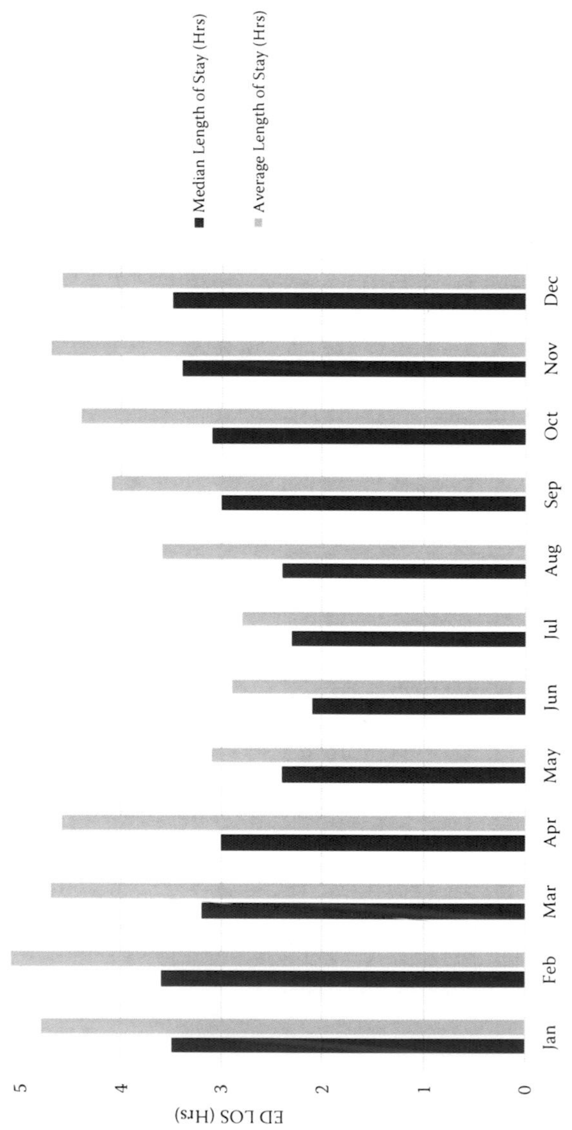

FIGURE 18.5
Grandview ED average and median LOS.

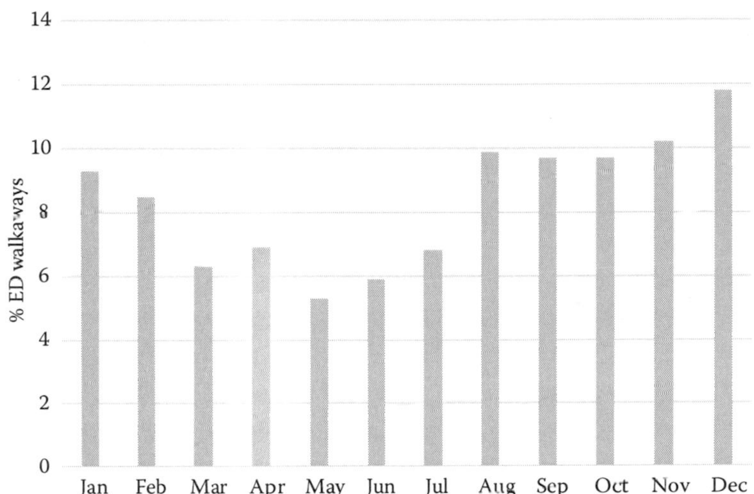

FIGURE 18.6
Grandview ED walkaways.

"Each silo is smaller and far less complex," Arnold says. "In fact, some divisions, such as IT, don't even exist. I like the papers you sent."*

"In 1950," I go on, "Grandview Hospital comprises comparatively few and shallow silos. How do these silos coordinate their activities?"

"Informally," says Madeleine. "Collegially."

I nod. "Now let's fast forward. Describe Grandview today."

"Many more silos," Madeleine says, "each deeper and much more complex. Oncology, for example, is a universe. Cancer care used to mean surgery and palliative care. Now there's chemotherapy, radiation, and various surgical options. Each of

* This chapter is informed by the work of my friend and colleague, Dr. Steven Spear. I recommend Dr. Spear's work, including his book, *Chasing the Rabbit* (New York: McGraw-Hill, 2009) and his articles in the *Harvard Business Review*.

these, in turn, has multiple subspecialties. Surgery, for example, includes laser, cryosurgery, electrosurgery, laparoscopy or robotic surgery, and that's just a partial list."

I walk to the whiteboard and start drawing. "How do these deep, complex, and numerous silos align their activities today?" (See Figure 18.7.)

Madeleine looks at me. "Our alignment process hasn't really changed. We're still aligning informally."

"That's why building our management system is Job One," Arnold says.

"Next question. How do complex systems *fail*?" I ask. "Think of the *Challenger* and *Columbia* space shuttle disasters. Think of Taylor Motor's bankruptcy six years ago."

Arnold shrugs. "I have no idea."

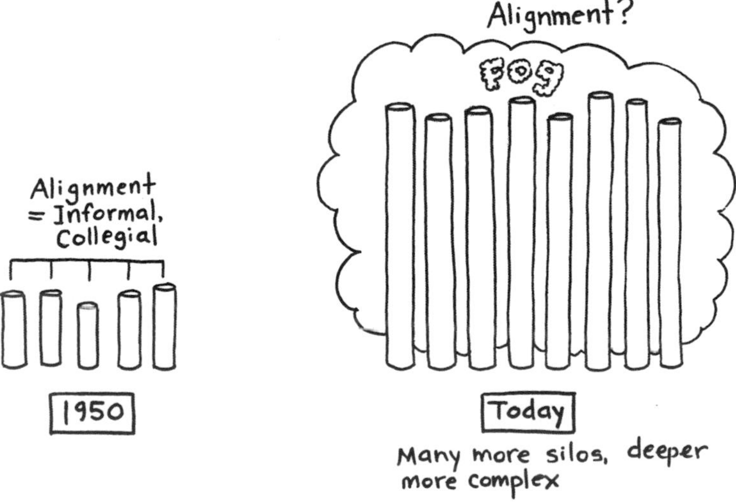

FIGURE 18.7
Grandview Hospital—then and now. Copyright 2015 Lean Pathways Inc.

"Complex systems fail the way a spider web fails—when the wrong combination of filaments fails, at the wrong time. This was true in the *Challenger* and *Columbia* space shuttle disasters, at Three Mile Island—and in Taylor Motors' bankruptcy. To avoid catastrophic failure, we need to fix broken filaments continually, as a spider does."

"Hold on," says Arnold. "In our Flow kaizen sessions you talked about Production Physics and the importance of managing bottlenecks. How does that fit in?"

"The weak-link-in-the-chain metaphor is helpful for Flow kaizen," I reply. "But it's not rich enough to describe complex systems such as the space shuttle, Grandview, or Taylor Motors. Let me repeat, such systems fail *when the wrong combination of filaments fails at the wrong time*. Next question: How do complex systems *succeed*?"

"Something about rules," says Arnold.

I nod again. "Think of complex natural systems. How does a flock of birds successfully migrate every year? By applying simple rules: *Don't hit anything. Stay in the middle of the flock. Try to go in the same direction as the other birds.*"

The implications hang there like ripe fruit (Figure 18.8).

"So by applying simple rules," Madeleine says, "we can create order in complex systems such as Grandview Hospital."

"A lot of people believe it takes bigger and faster computers," Arnold says.

"Would bigger, faster computers have prevented the oncology bag problem, or the NICU near-tragedy?" I ask.

Silence.

"There are Four Rules," I continue, "corresponding to Standards, Connections, Pathways, and Improvement. Rules 1, 2, and 3 tell you where the spider web is broken. Rule 4 tells you how to fix it. The Grandview web is big and complex. Murphy's

FIGURE 18.8
How complex systems fail—and succeed. Copyright 2015 Lean Pathways Inc.

Law rules the universe—filaments keep breaking at unexpected times and in ever-changing combinations." (See Figure 18.9.)

"Hence, Total Involvement," Madeleine offers. "Everybody has to continually respond to abnormalities and fix broken filaments, as you call them."

"The Four Rules inform everything we've learned up till now," I tell them. "Each Rule builds on the last. We begin by standardizing points in our system—*Point kaizen.* Then we connect standardized processes within a department or line of care—*Flow kaizen.* Finally, we define the pathways along which patients and support services flow—*System kaizen.*"

"Which parallels Levels 1, 2, and 3 checking and our management system," Arnold says. "Point kaizen is front line work; Flow kaizen the work of senior managers and directors; and System kaizen, our work."

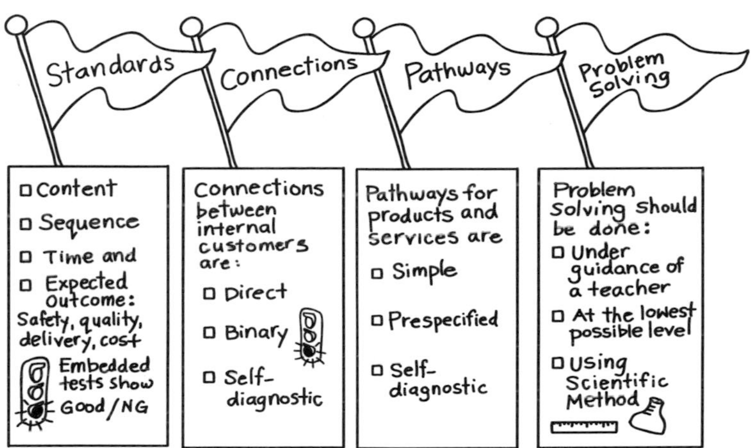

FIGURE 18.9
The Four Rules. Copyright 2015 Lean Pathways Inc.

"More or less," I reply. "As we'll see today, our front line folks are fully capable of doing Flow and even System kaizen. The senior leader's job is to enable them by removing hassles and maintaining constancy of purpose."

"The river metaphor again," Arnold puts in.

"What do you mean by self-diagnostic?" Madeleine asks.

"Each rule contains embedded tests," I respond. "In fact, that's your homework: Find as many embedded tests as you can in the Four Rules."

"Leadership," I go on, "is a process of *discovery*—not compliance. Let me quote Andy Saito: *What did we discover is broken today? How did we fix it? How do we share the learning?* Andy calls this the remedy for Big Company Disease."

Madeleine and Arnold are silent again. "Rules 1 and 2 make perfect sense," says Arnold. "Rule 3 seems abstract. Can you tell me more about pathways?"

"We need to understand the structure of demand," I say, "the content and daily, weekly, and seasonal patterns. Then we can segment demand and align our resources accordingly. We seek to reduce variation and keep asset utilization (doctor, nurse, beds, and so on) under 80 percent.

"Take a simple system like the Humpty Dumpty, my parent's restaurant. My folks understand daily, weekly, and seasonal demand and have developed flexible capacity to satisfy it. They've segmented demand in useful ways—high runners and low runners, hots and colds, and their kitchen layout reflects it. High runners such as sandwiches and hamburgers tend to have lower production cycle times and relatively low demand variation. The customer's cycle time is also low. At lunch time, people want their sandwiches quickly. So my folks have a designated "high runner pathway," a line that really moves.

"By contrast, low runners such as steak tartare have longer cycle times and much higher demand variation. My parents instinctively set up a 'low runner pathway' too. Thereby they maximize throughput while minimizing delay."

"I get it," says Arnold. "Rule 3 means understand demand, segment it, and then align your resources."

"We have a lot of obstacles there," Madeleine says. "I'll bet our utilizations on night shift are crazy."

"You're right," I tell her. "Extreme LOS numbers coincide with excessive nurse, doctor, and bed utilization rates. Aligning capacity and demand are a critical countermeasure. Developing flexible capacity, like my folks do, is another.

"The Four Rules inform every element of the Toyota system," I continue. "Toyota methods make problems, broken web filaments, *visible*—so that we can fix them. We're never finished. Andy says improvement is endless and eternal. Speak of the devil, here he is."

Andy smiles and says hello, and we head into the ED. Tony Pica and Uma Singh, ED director and chief ED nurse, respectively, are waiting for us. They're especially happy to see Andy, who kids with them good-naturedly.

"ED processes have three main components," Tony begins, "Door to Doc, Doc to Disposition, and Disposition to Discharge. Each comprises multiple pathways, as you know. We're focusing on the Door to Doc segment, the most important for patient satisfaction.

"Here's our current process," Tony goes on, walking to a white board. "As you can see, there's plenty of transport, delay, and overprocessing waste. Our main resources—nurses, doctors, and beds—can get overwhelmed during peak demand." (See Figure 18.10.)

"Most of our patients are nonacute," Uma adds. "Segmenting them is the key to flow and patient satisfaction. Their symptoms are typically fever, cough, stomach, or back pain—stuff we can

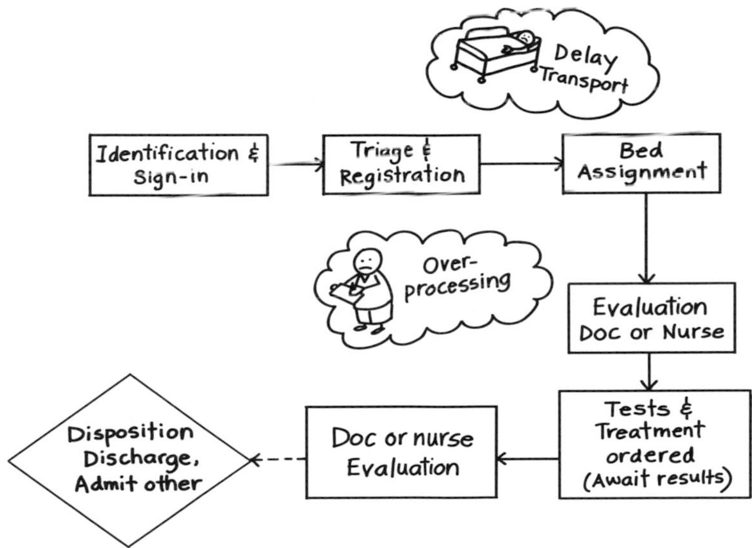

FIGURE 18.10
Current ED Door to Doc process. Copyright 2015 Lean Pathways Inc.

deal with quickly. So we're piloting a Fast Track for Level 4 and 5 patients." We're directing Level 1, 2, and 3 patients to a Rapid Assessment team.

"Mr. Saito calls Levels 4 and 5 our 'high runners.' Treating them requires less work and shorter cycle times and they expect quick diagnosis and treatment. Our targets are thirty minutes for Door to Doc and sixty minutes for total length of stay."

"Ambitious," Madeleine says. "Our current numbers are twice that."

"We're piloting a Fast Track pathway for nonacute patients," says Tony. "Let's go see it." (See Figure 18.11.)

Tony and Uma take us to the Fast Track area and introduce the pilot leader, a young fellow named Jake Stiles. He, too, is happy to see Andy.

"We've combined Identification and Triage," Jake tells us. "Our peak demand is twenty patients per hour and our Takt* time is three minutes. We're in the midst of a standardized work kaizen. We use Takt time for nonacute patients. For acute patients, clinicians give us target cycle times."

"Three-minute cycle times, that's quite a challenge," Madeleine says.

"Our pilot process entails a quick look and assignment," says Jake. "We removed a lot of waste, and moved registration and other stuff downstream. The latter gave us a boost in patient satisfaction. People hate having to answer payment questions before they've been seen."

"So doctors, nurses, and beds can all be bottlenecks," Arnold says. "What are you doing about it?"

"Mr. Saito has taught us to run experiments. We make a hypothesis, observe what happens, and adjust. As problems arise, we ping them off and update our standard work. We've got some nice

* Takt = Available time ÷ Demand = 60 minutes ÷ 20 patients = 3 minutes.

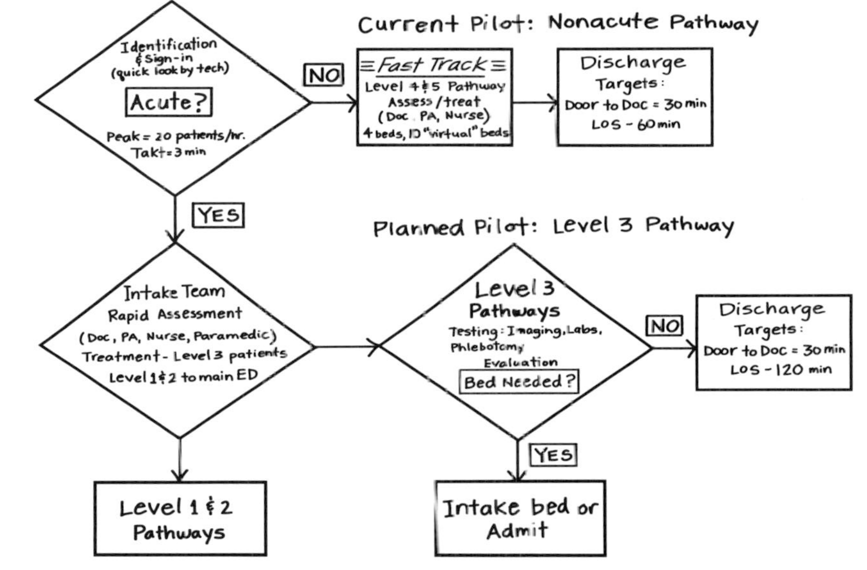

FIGURE 18.11
Pilot ED Door to Doc process. Copyright 2015 Lean Pathways Inc.

countermeasures. Like using physician assistants where possible to free up doctors. And using 'virtual beds' for vertical* patients. Our Fast Track area has a place for people to sit while we do testing and treating. They don't mind as long as we get to them quick."

"How about nursing bottlenecks?" Madeleine asks.

"Current shift schedules are a problem," Uma says. "They're misaligned with our peak demand periods, which are around 11:00 a.m. and 11:00 p.m. It's a touchy subject, especially after all the layoffs."

"You've told us about Standards and Pathways, Rules 1 and 3. What about Rule 2—Connections?" Arnold asks.

"Our most important connections are with our main service providers—Imaging, Labs, and Phlebotomy. Each has a daily team huddle, which one of us attends. They know our target throughput and turnaround times. They also attend our daily huddle. It's taken a while to build trust."

"What kind of results are you getting, Jake?" Arnold asks.

Jake takes us to the Fast Track team board. Door-to-Doc time, LOS and Walkaways were down 30, 24, and 23 percent, respectively.

"Not bad," Arnold says. "What's next?"

"We need to build some flexible capacity in our Fast Track line," Jake replies. "We also want to pilot ESI Level 3 pathways. We've got some flow improvement ideas. For example, assigned seating at Imaging and Phlebotomy for vertical patients waiting for test results. Or a 'Green Room' with leather recliners, flat-screen TV, and a mini-nursing station where patients and providers could discuss results and give discharge instructions as needed. The idea is to make our queues more visible."

We thank Tony, Uma, and Jake and walk back to a conference room for reflections and learnings. Arnold goes first.

* Patients who are able to walk.

"Like Mr. Saito says, everything is connected. Standards, Connections, and Pathways make problems visible. Pathways for Level 4 and 5 nonacute patients allow us to see what's happening across the ED."

"Pathways are made of Standards and Connections," Madeleine says. "We have Pathways for things such as Code Trauma, Code Sepsis, or Code Stroke. But we need them for Level 5, 4, and 3 patients too."

"Understand and stratify demand. Align capacity to demand," says Arnold. "That's a big one."

"Mistrust corrodes improvement," says Madeleine. "We have to regain the trust of ED nurses."

"It will take time," Andy says. "They have worked in a difficult system for a long time."

I think of Doreen, the ED director, who was honest with me all those months ago. She has since left Grandview.

"We haven't talked about Rule 4," Arnold says.

That's next, I tell him.

Study Questions

1. The Four Rules are full of embedded tests. Identify as many as you can. Sketch out your answer using as few written words as possible.
2. Give three examples of embedded tests in
   a. Your workplace (e.g., a temperature sensor in a hospital autoclave sterilizer)
   b. Outside work (e.g., a necessary field in an online form)
3. Give three examples of direct, binary connections between a customer and a supplier
   a. At work (e.g., a digital replenishment signal between a consumer goods distribution center and the retailer's shelf)

   b. Outside of work (e.g., ordering a laptop computer online directly from the manufacturer)
4. Give three examples of simple, prespecified pathways
   a. At work (e.g., standardized material delivery route)
   b. Outside of work (e.g., bus service)
5. What does self-diagnostic mean? Sketch it out.

19

Practical Problem Solving

Rules 1, 2, and 3 make problems visible. Rule 4 is about fixing them. For our next Executive Coaching module, Practical Problem Solving, Carol Kwan and Bill McKnight meet me in a conference room outside of perhaps our most daunting *gemba*.

Grandview Surgical Services department is world famous and comprises

- 29 staffed operating rooms
- 25,000 surgeries per year
- Twelve specialties including cardiac, oncology, neuro, orthopedics, spine, vascular, general, plastics, thoracic, transplant, otolaryngology, and ophthalmology

Surgical Services is also a key to filling in Grandview's structural deficit. "Operating Room flow is a gold mine," says Arnold.

I am in awe of our surgical teams. I've watched them give sight to a blind woman, with Dr. McKnight beside me explaining the retinal prosthesis surgery. I watched them work *ex vivo* on a diseased liver and on cancerous lungs. I watched a heart transplant. In each case, the patient lived and was transformed.

Their brilliance and gallantry is in sharp contrast to the hassles that afflict them—missing lab tests, wrong and missing

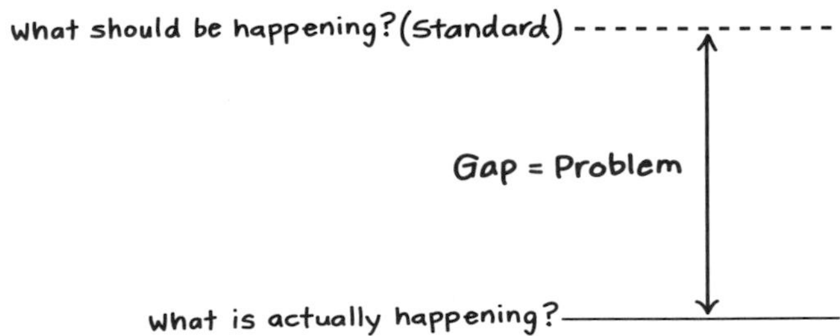

FIGURE 19.1
What is a problem?

equipment, contaminated equipment, mislabeling, poor layouts, and the like.

"Complex systems fail the way a spider web fails," I start in, "and succeed as a spider web does—when we continually fix the broken filaments, the countless problems that arise. Rule 4 says: 'We solve problems at the lowest possible level following the scientific method.' So, *what is a problem?*" (See Figure 19.1.)

"A problem is a deviation from a standard," Carol says. "I like that. It's cut and dried."

"No standard, no problem," Dr. McKnight adds.

"And what is a standard?" I ask.

"A picture of what should be happening," they chime.

I sketch it out.

"TPS* is about making problems visible," I continue. "Strategy Deployment is about creating problems by setting aggressive targets. So here we are surrounded by problems. Now what?

"We need a simple and sound problem solving *drill* that we teach everybody. At Taylor Motors, we began with an eight-step process, experimented with Toyota's seven-step process, and

* Toyota Production System.

finally boiled it all down to four steps. Four-step problem solving works on manufacturing, supply chain, and design problems, and on for Point, Flow, and System problems."

I sketch this one out too (Figure 19.2).

1. Do I have a problem?
    - What should be happening?
    - What is actually happening?
    - So what? Why is this important? How does it relate to True North?
2. Do I know the cause?
    - Point of cause (discovery)
    - Direct cause
    - Root cause

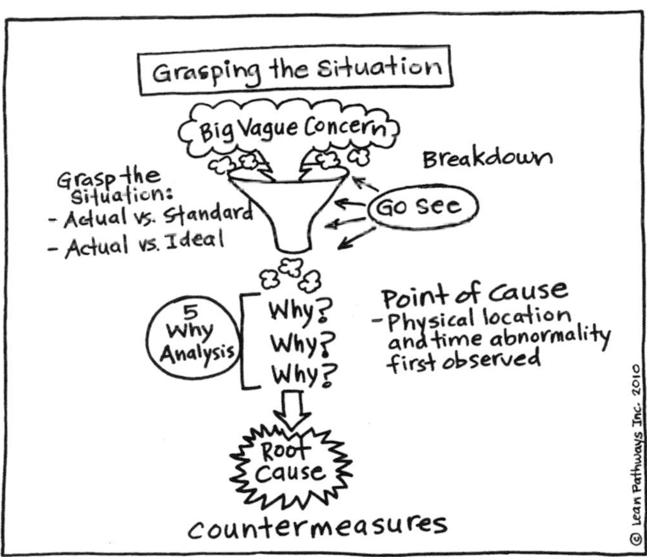

FIGURE 19.2
Practical problem solving—the Four Steps. Copyright 2015 Lean Pathways Inc.

3. Have I confirmed cause and effect?
    - Can I observe cause and effect directly?
    - If not, what experiments will we run?
4. Have I confirmed the countermeasure?
    - How will we lock in the new standard?
    - How will we check to ensure we're still following it in 30/60/90 days?

"Here's the underlying algorithm," I tell them. "Recognize it?" (See Figure 19.3.)

"Same one we use to develop our strategy A3s," says Carol.

"Anybody know what a fractal is?" I ask.

"Chaos theory," Bill replies. "A fractal is a continuously recurring pattern at smaller and smaller levels of magnification."

"TPS is full of fractals," I say. "Here's some homework for you. What other TPS fractals can you identify? Let's

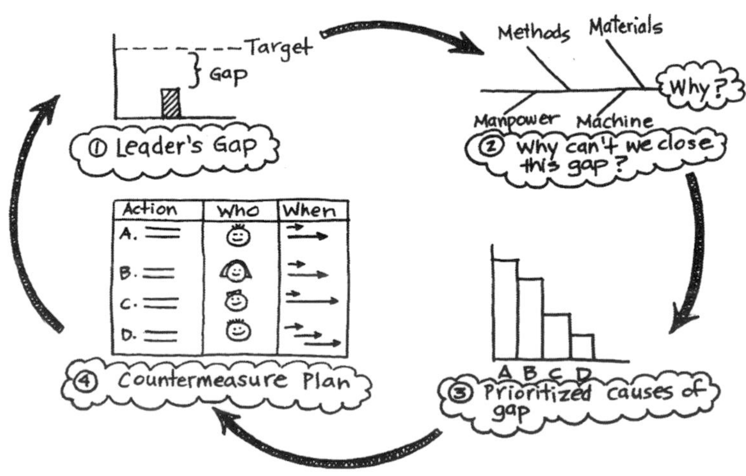

FIGURE 19.3
Problem-solving algorithm. Copyright 2015 Lean Pathways Inc.

continue. Rule 4 is self-diagnostic. What are the embedded tests?"

Carol and Bill mull it over.

"Has the team member defined 'what should be happening'," says Carol, "and 'what's actually happening'?"

"Is the gap linked to True North?" Bill puts in.

"Really, all the questions you drew out are tests," Carol says.

I nod. "Now let's go see Surgical Services."

Nate Friedman and Melissa Meaghan, Surgical Services and Nursing directors, respectively, are waiting for us.

"We would like to show you some of our problem-solving activity," Nate says. "Bennie Walton and the Breakout team have been a great help. Our focus is reducing delay, improving throughput, and reducing infections. Our key metrics are

- Turnaround time (close to cut)—time between last patient leaving the OR and the start of the next operation
- First Case Start—percentage of first scheduled cases that start at the designated time
- Cancellation rate
- Throughput—A, B, and C surgeries completed each day. A, B, and C categories are determined by the complexity and frequency of the surgery
- Catheter-associated blood stream infections (CABSI), measured as CABSI per 1000 trips for our ICUs and CABSI per 1000 catheter days for Grandview overall."

Nate leads us to the Zone 1 team board. "Our focus here is reducing delay on the day of surgery. Here's our existing process." (See Figure 19.4.)

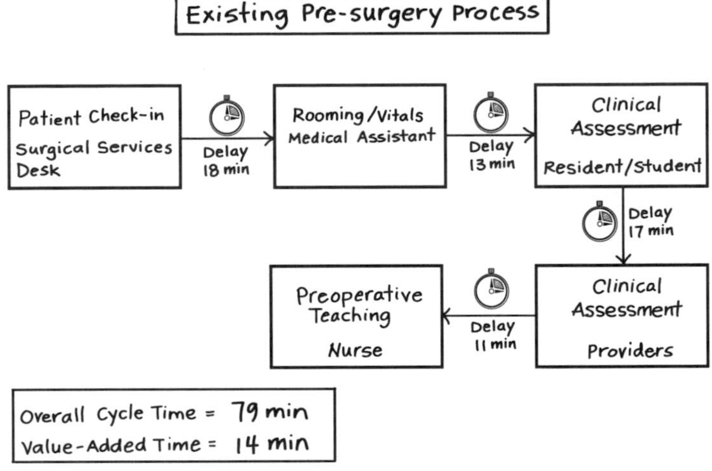

FIGURE 19.4
Current pre-surgery process. Copyright 2015 Lean Pathways Inc.

"Lots of waste, as you can see," says Nate. "Let me take you through our thinking.

1. *Do we have a problem?*
   a. Yes—pre-surgery cycle time is seventy-nine minutes; target is thirty-seven minutes.
   b. So what? Reducing delay and improving throughput is one of our core objectives.
2. *Do we know the cause?*
   a. We drew out our process and measured cycle times.
   b. We found delay and over-processing waste—multiple information forms, and multiple people copying and recopying information. The patient gets more and more anxious.

3. *Have we confirmed cause and effect?*
    a. Partially. Our pilot process addresses the observed hassles, but not enough to achieve a target cycle time of thirty-seven minutes. (See Figure 19.5.)
    b. Current pilot process cycle times are forty-nine minutes, a nice improvement, but still off our target. We're missing something.
4. *Have we confirmed countermeasures?*
    a. Not yet. We've decided to go with our new process and have drafted standardized work including consolidated forms. We'll have to train everybody and continue to track results on our team board."

"Any idea why the new process isn't meeting target cycle times?" Bill asks.

"Not sure we've adequately prepared MAs," Melissa says. "There's also some confusion about the consolidated form."

"Still, a nice Point improvement," says Carol. "Are you doing any Flow kaizen?"

"Yes we are," says Melissa. "In fact, this work is part of a Flow kaizen aimed at increasing surgical throughput to 29,000

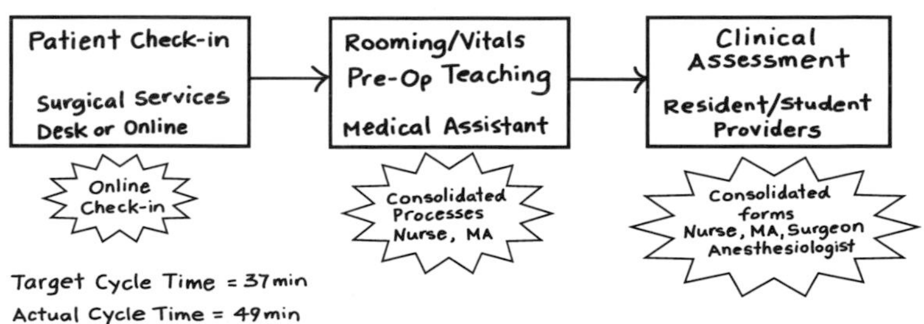

FIGURE 19.5
Pilot pre-surgery process. Copyright 2015 Lean Pathways Inc.

surgeries per year, by the end of next year. We've found that our biggest obstacles are

- Delay
  - Pre-surgery
  - OR changeover; we have a joint project with Housekeeping here
  - Wrong and missing stuff in surgical kits—Steve Yablonski's Medical Instrument Reprocessing team has this one.
- Surgery cancellations
  - Team 3 is working with the labs on this one. Late test results are the biggest causes of cancellation.
- Demand—can we fill freed up capacity?
  - Our marketing team has that one.

"To be honest," Nate says. "Flow kaizen is a big stretch for us. We're not good at coordinating multiple teams toward a common goal. We've always worked in silos."

"Flow kaizen and Level 2 work in general are weak links in our management system," I say. "Connecting the silos will take time."

"The nice thing is now we have time for this kind of work," Melissa says. "We're no longer doing silly state-driven stuff."

"Any other work you can tell us about?" Carol asks.

"We're studying the CABSI problem," Nate says. "We think anesthesiologists may be a major source of contamination because of hand hygiene and IV line contamination. There's some tension there, as you can imagine, but we have the data.

"We're also piloting a new Surgical Safety Assessment," Melissa adds. "Everybody's been involved—surgeons, anesthesiologists, nurses, and even patients. We're using the 'challenge and response' approach. It's a big cultural change for us. We're getting a lot of flak."

"From who, pray tell?" Dr. McKnight asks.

"You know who," says Melissa.

* *

A few days later I run into Brewster's bodyguard, Lester, in the garden near the rear 24th Street entrance. Early evening, dayshift staff have gone home. I often linger here before taking the subway home. Lester must have been waiting for me.

Lester sticks his face into mine. "They say you're a big martial arts guy. But I think you're a wuss."

There's nobody around. If he's going to attack me, it's a good time.

"Brewster is trying to discredit me, isn't he, Lester? He figures if you and I get into a fight, he'll have things to talk about on his TV show."

Lester keeps glowering.

"But you know," I tell him, "I expected something like this. So I talked to my friend Clarence Martin, Grandview's director of security. I expressed my concerns and asked them to keep an eye out for you. I suspect we're on camera right now. So you can go ahead and attack me. I'll defend myself and have you charged with assault. Do you really want a criminal record?"

Lester blinks. "No, I don't."

"Then get the hell out of here."

I tell Sarah about it when I get home. My heart has stopped racing. Luckily, Lester believed me when I told him there were cameras in the garden. Sarah pours us some wine and we go out on to the balcony to take in the city.

"How bizarre," she says. "I'm so glad you didn't take the bait."

"Chiba-sensei says 'win without fighting.' It's counterintuitive for me."

Sarah cups my face in her hands. "You're still a warrior. You just found a better way to win."

Study Questions

1. According to Rule 4, problem solving should be done at "the lowest possible level."
   a. What's wrong with having a centralized team of specialists that solves problems as they arise?
   b. Are front line team members in your organization capable of solving Point, Flow, and/or System problems? Explain your answer with examples.
2. What are the embedded tests in Rule 4?
3. Define Point, Flow, and System kaizen.
4. Assess problem solving in your organization at
   a. Level 1—front line
   b. Level 2—middle and upper middle managers
   c. Level 3—senior leaders
   d. What could your organization do to improve problem solving at each level?
5. What does "confirm countermeasures" mean? Provide examples.
6. What is the scientific method? Sketch it out.

20

Year-End Review

Late fall melancholy, trees bare, flowers gone, a year since we buried Uncle Angie. We file out of St. Irene's Greek Orthodox Church and head to the Boy on a Dolphin banquet hall near Astoria Park. It's *Psychosavato*, a Saturday dedicated to the souls of the departed.

Billy and George escort their Mom, Aunt Jennie, to the waiting car. George is carrying a tray of *kollyva*—boiled wheat prepared with sugar, walnuts, cinnamon, and other spices. Wheat represents the life cycle of death and regeneration and *kollyva* the soul of the deceased and everlasting life. It's been a hard year for the family. Jennie's bearing up better than her boys.

Everybody makes a fuss about Sarah, pinching her cheeks and telling her she's too thin. It's about time, they say to me. Our girls, Sophie and Helen, are thrilled about having a little brother or sister, belying all my worries. During lunch I sit next to my Dad, who is in top form.

"ANGIE," I told him, "YOU HAVE TO KILL ALL THE ROACHES!"

"No," he says, "just most of them."

"AFTER A FEW LAWSUITS, ANGIE SEES THE LIGHT. NICK, HE SAYS TO ME, YOU WERE RIGHT. THEN HE HAS ANOTHER BRAINWAVE AND STARTS BUYING UP

CONDEMNED COUCHES AND MATTRESSES! NICK, HE SAYS, I'LL FUMIGATE AND MAKE A FORTUNE!"

Hard to believe Nick Papas was ever worried about anything.

* *

A few weeks later we have our Grandview year-end review with Gwen Carter and Rachel Armstrong in attendance. All our True North metrics have improved, many by double digits. In our pilot zones, we've improved by more than 20 percent across the board. Our net operating loss is down from $66 million to less than $30 million. Arnold said there are other things at work, but TPS* is a central factor.

Our management system is taking root. Our pilot zones have working Level 1 and Level 2 huddles in almost all zones. We've implemented 374 Quick & Easy kaizens and done forty-seven focused kaizen events. Our Lean Coordinator Network has grown to more than a hundred members. One-on-one coaching with the core management team is shifting core mental models.

"Well done," Rachel says. "Grandview Hospital has come further in one year than many manufacturing plants."

"We have superb senseis," Madeleine Harper says.

"I'm pleased and impressed," says Gwen Carter, "and looking forward to next year. Now, I'd like to hear from our senseis. Tom, Andy, how did we do this year?"

Andy and I present our feedback gently, providing specific examples for each point. Overall, we're pleased. The team's progress exceeded our expectations. We give a tip of the hat to the core management team—John, Madeleine, Arnold, Bill, Carol, and Pinky, and to Danny Kaufman and the Breakout team.

"We're building a foundation," I tell them. "Our improvement work the past year has been mostly at the Point level.

* Toyota Production System.

We've made a handful of Flow improvements and almost no System kaizen. That's next year's work.

"Key Thinkers haven't really grasped the situation in our focus areas," I continue. "Deployment to the front line is dodgy. Standards outside of the pilot areas are all over the place. We're just beginning to connect our silos. We've not yet engaged our physicians."

"Thinking is beginning to change," Andy adds, "but we are still hiding problems. Problem solving is not so good. Leaders are most comfortable telling team members what to do. We like jumping to countermeasures."

Gwen then asks the CEO, COO, CFO, CMO, CMO, and CSO for reflections and learning points.

"Strategy is about saying no," John Fox says. "That's my biggest lesson."

"I looked in the mirror," says Madeleine, "and I saw the problem. We have splendid human capital but we're not using it. I'm grateful to Tom and Andy for helping me understand that."

"TPS is just good management," says Arnold. "Lean means don't be a dumbass. The hard part is staying the course. One-on-one coaching is critical for us. Tom, Andy, and the Taylor senseis have given us a big boost."

"Our management system is the key," Bill McKnight puts in. "Connected checking, run the business, improve the business—it's beginning to make sense. Looking forward to next year."

"Connections—Rule 2," Carol offers, "that's the big one for me. We have to connect the silos. We have to think horizontally, from the patient's point of view. It's a huge shift for us."

"'Go see'," Pinky says. "I was afraid to go to the front line. But that's how you get to understand your current condition. You have to zoom in and then zoom out. Your strategy doesn't have to be perfect. Deployment, engaging people, is the most important thing."

Gwen Carter thanks everyone for their efforts the past year. "Well done," she says, "and full speed ahead!"

* *

Andy and I have dinner that night at the Blue Iguana. We begin with bourbon, Knob Hill and Pappy Van Winkle, respectively, and reflect on the past year.

"The stars and planets aligned for us, sensei."

Andy nods. "We have been fortunate."

We click glasses.

"You are a sensei now, Tom-san," he tells me.

"Maybe in a small way, thanks to you."

We look out onto the sea of humanity that is Broadway. Grandview Hospital takes care of these people, and gives them the greatest gift of all—health, time, life.

Grandview has transformed me. It's a healing place, after all. A year ago I was depressed, confused, and only partially available for my family. Dr. Vogel has helped me understand the roots of my discontent. I've posted an image of Atlas in my office.

"Our Grandview contract runs for another year," I say. "What do we do then?"

Andy smiles. "There is much opportunity, Tom-san."

* *

A few weeks later Sarah and I go into Grandview for our first ultrasound appointment. Sarah is entering her third trimester, and after some initial morning sickness, is doing well. Amniocentesis suggests the baby is developing normally—no genetic abnormalities, thank God. Today we'll check Mama and baby health and learn the sex of our child.

The Imaging team kibitz and make jokes. Are we flowing yet, Tom? Something's flowing, I tell them. Shelley, the shift

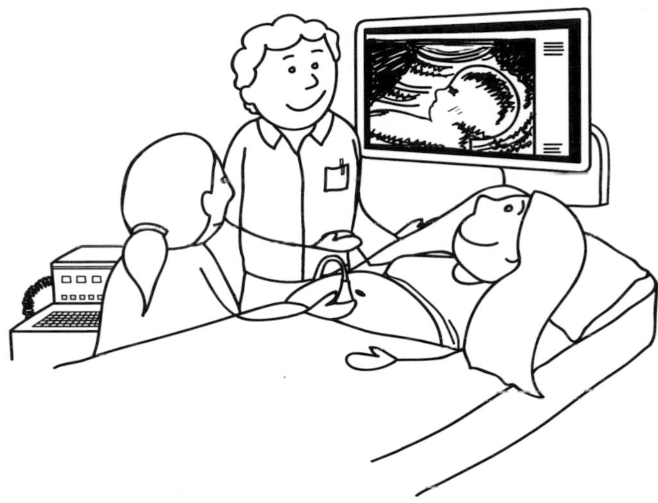

FIGURE 20.1
Our little boy. Copyright 2015 Lean Pathways Inc.

supervisor, stops by to say hello. It feels good in here—a professional team on top of its game.

Sarah lies on the examination table. The technician, Samantha, spreads gel over Sarah's abdomen and lays the transducer on top.

"We're getting something," Samantha says. She scans the monitor carefully. "Everything looks good."

"Can I see?" asks Sarah, holding back tears.

Samantha turns the screen toward us. There's our little boy (Figure 20.1).

Study Questions

1. What are three things you learned in reading this book? Sketch them out.
2. Describe three ways you'll apply the lessons learned in this book.

3. In your experience, what are the biggest obstacles to breakthrough improvement in a hospital (or in any large organization)?
   a. What are the root causes of each obstacle?
   b. What are possible countermeasures?
4. What are the biggest obstacles to sustained improvement in *your* organization?
   a. What are the root causes of each obstacle?
   b. What are possible countermeasures?
5. Madeleine Harper says, "I looked into the mirror and saw the problem."
   a. Do you agree or disagree with her? Explain your answer.
   b. What is senior leadership's role in an organizational transformation?
   c. In your experience, what prevents senior leaders from fulfilling this role?
   d. What are possible countermeasures?

Index

G

U